The Pure Good of Theory

THE BUCKNELL LECTURES IN LITERARY THEORY
General Editors: Michael Payne and Harold Schweizer

The lectures in this series explore some of the fundamental changes in literary studies that have occurred during the past thirty years in response to new work in feminism, Marxism, psychoanalysis, and deconstruction. They assess the impact of these changes and examine specific texts in the light of this new work. Each volume in the series includes a critical assessment of the lecturer's own publications, an interview, and a comprehensive bibliography.

Frank Kermode   *Poetry, Narrative, History*
Terry Eagleton   *The Significance of Theory*
Toril Moi   *Feminist Theory and Simone de Beauvoir*
J. Hillis Miller   *Hawthorne and History*
Christopher Norris   *Spinoza and the Origins of Modern*
                       Critical Theory
Denis Donoghue   *The Pure Good of Theory*

The Pure Good of Theory

Denis Donoghue

BLACKWELL
Oxford UK & Cambridge USA

First published 1992

Blackwell Publishers
Three Cambridge Center
Cambridge, Massachusetts 02142
USA

108 Cowley Road
Oxford OX4 1JF
UK

Library of Congress Cataloging-in-Publication Data
Donoghue, Denis.
    The pure good of theory / Denis Donoghue.
        p.   cm. — (The Bucknell lectures in literary theory)
    Includes bibliographical references and index.
    ISBN 0–631–18474–0. — ISBN 0–631–18475–9
    1. Criticism.   2. Literature—History and criticism—Theory, etc.
I. Title.   II. Series.
PN81.D585   1992
801'.951—dc20   91–39574
                                                              CIP

British Library Cataloguing in Publication Data

A CIP catalogue record for this book is available from the British Library.

Typeset in 11 on 13 pt Plantin
by Photo·graphics, Honiton, Devon
Printed in Great Britain by Biddles Ltd., Guildford.

This book is printed on acid-free paper

Contents

Preface

Fundamental and far-reaching changes in literary studies, often compared to paradigmatic shifts in the sciences, have been taking place during the last thirty years. These changes have included enlarging the literary canon not only to include novels, poems, and plays by writers whose race, gender, or nationality had marginalized their work, but also to include texts by philosophers, psychoanalysts, historians, anthropologists, social and religious thinkers, who previously were studied by critics merely as 'background'. The stance of the critic and student of literature is also now more in question than ever before. In 1951 it was possible for Cleanth Brooks to declare with confidence that the critic's job was to describe and evaluate literary objects, implying the relevance for criticism of the model of scientific objectivity while leaving unasked questions concerning significant issues in scientific theory, such as complementarity, indeterminacy, and the use of metaphor. Now the possibility of value-free scepticism is itself in doubt as many feminist, Marxist, and psychoanalytic theorists have stressed the inescapability of ideology and the consequent obligation of teachers and students of literature to declare their political, axiological, and aesthetic positions in order to make those positions conscious and available for examination. Such expansion and deepening of literary studies has, for many critics, revitalized their field.

Those for whom the theoretical revolution has been regenerative would readily echo, and apply to criticism, Lacan's call to revitalize psychoanalysis: 'I consider it to be an urgent task to disengage from concepts that are being deadened by routine use the meaning that they regain both from a re-examination of their history and from a reflexion on their subjective foundations. That, no doubt, is the teacher's prime function.'

Many practising writers and teachers of literature, however, see recent developments in literary theory as dangerous and anti-humanistic. They would insist that displacement of the centrality of the word, claims for the 'death of the author', emphasis upon gaps and incapacities in language, and indiscriminate opening of the canon threaten to marginalize literature itself. In this view the advance of theory is possible only because of literature's retreat in the face of aggressive moves by Marxism, feminism, deconstruction, and psychoanalysis. Furthermore, at a time of militant conservatism and the dominance of corporate values in America and Western Europe, literary theory threatens to diminish further the declining audience for literature and criticism. Theoretical books are difficult to read; they usually assume that their readers possess knowledge that few have who have received a traditional literary education; they often require massive reassessments of language, meaning, and the world; they seem to draw their life from suspect branches of other disciplines: professional philosophers usually avoid Derrida; psychoanalysts dismiss Freud as unscientific; Lacan was excommunicated by the International Psycho-Analytical Association.

The volumes in this series record part of the attempt at Bucknell University to sustain conversation about changes in literary studies, the impact of those changes on literary art, and the significance of literary theory for the humanities and human sciences. A generous grant from the Andrew W. Mellon Foundation has made possible a five-year series of visiting lectureships by internationally known participants in the reshaping of literary studies. Each volume includes a comprehensive introduction to the published work of the lecturer, the Bucknell Lectures, an interview, and a comprehensive bibliography.

The editors would like to express their gratitude to the participants in the faculty seminars on literary theory for their unfailing support of this project.

ACKNOWLEDGEMENTS

Grateful acknowledgement is made for permission to reprint from the following previously published material: From *Opus Posthumous* by Wallace Stevens, edit. Samuel French Morse. Copyright © 1957 by Elsie Stevens and Holly Stevens. Reprinted by permission of Alfred A. Knopf, Inc. and Faber and Faber Limited. From *The Collected Poems of Wallace Stevens* Copyright © 1954 by Wallace Stevens, reprinted by permission of Alfred A. Knopf, Inc. and Faber and Faber Limited. Poetry by William Butler Yeats reprinted with permission of Macmillan Publishing Company from *The Collected Poems of W. B. Yeats: A New Edition*, edited by Richard J. Finneran: 'Politics'. Copyright © 1940 by Georgie Yeats, renewed 1968 by Bertha Georgie Yeats, Michael Butler Yeats, and Anne Yeats; excerpt from 'Among School Children' Copyright © 1928 by Macmillan Publishing Company, renewed 1956 by Georgie Yeats. Excerpt from 'High Windows' from *High Windows* by Philip Larkin. Copyright © 1974 by Philip Larkin. Reprinted by permission of Farrar, Straus & Giroux, Inc. and Faber and Faber Limited. Excerpt from 'Against *Ulysses*' by Leo Bersani. Copyright © 1988 *Raritan: A Quarterly Review*, reprinted with permission. Excerpt from *Watt* by Samuel Beckett, published © 1959 by Grove Press, reprinted with permission of Grove Weidenfeld and Calder Publications Limited. Excerpt from 'Animula' from *Collected Poems, 1909–1962*, by T. S. Eliot, copyright 1936 by Harcourt Brace Jovanovich, Inc. and copyright © 1964, 1963 by T. S. Eliot, reprinted by permission of the publisher and Faber and Faber Limited. Excerpts from *The Reform of Education* by Giovanni Gentile and translated by Dino Bigongiari, reprinted by permission of Harcourt Brace Jovanovich, Inc.

Introduction

In the concluding chapter of *Ferocious Alphabets* (1981), Denis Donoghue states that 'the conflict among the alphabets of criticism today turns upon the question of imagination' (p.208). It might also be said that the conflicts within Donoghue's own criticism have always turned upon the question of imagination, and that the resulting tension has been most fruitful for his work.

In *The Ordinary Universe* (1968), one of his earlier studies on the relationship between reality and the imagination, his starting point is an attack on those formalist critics who see the work of art as a verbal icon, separate from the messy and unaesthetic world of ordinary things; while granting the virtues of formalism, Donoghue wants to re-establish the connection between 'values, attitudes, motives, choice, preference, commitments' and 'speech, literature, the artifact, "the poem itself"' (*OU*, p. 16). The tension suggested here between concern for values and attention to pure form is really an expression of a deeper 'rivalry between the world and the word', or of that 'between the persuasions of the natural world and the structure of one's own imagination, between Ordinary things and Supreme Fictions' (*OU*, p. 17).

Clearly, in that book Donoghue is on the side of ordinary things. He admires Lawrence's poems, for example, because they 'rebuke the imperial imagination' (*OU*, p. 22). He quotes John Crowe Ransom with approval: 'we regard the endless mysterious fullness of this object, and respect the dignity of its objective existence after all – in spite of the ambition to mastery that has become more and more habitual with us' (*OU*, p. 22). Such an attitude to things is 'pious, poetic, never predatory' (*OU*, p. 23). 'Predatory' and 'imperial' are strong words, as is 'pious', and it soon becomes clear that what is being predated is not merely the realm of things in their objective reality; Donoghue is not mounting a naïve defence of realism; he is concerned with much larger issues. 'I would argue that existence, being, and fact are valuable because they are sponsored by something properly if loosely called an intention, and by an intention properly if loosely called divine; what Buber calls "the speech of God articulated in things and events"' (*OU*, p. 61).

To behave, therefore, with proper reverence before things and events is to acknowledge the realm of the divine, and Donoghue's quarrel with many modern writers is that, through their cult of the autonomous imagination, they turn away 'from the phenomenal world, they represent the Nietzschean imagination, virtually identified with the will' (*OU*, p. 64). Later, in *Thieves of Fire* (1974), he will call this the Promethean imagination, and in *The Sovereign Ghost* (1976), the angelic imagination. Of the three terms, 'angelic' is perhaps the most favourable, and indeed, as we shall see, the position taken in *The Ordinary Universe* receives considerable modification in the later writings. But even 'angelic' carries the overtone of 'fallen', and such an exercise of the imagination is still 'an act of will, it is alienated from the world and therefore whirls between two worlds, depending upon its own intensity to keep it going; scornful of existence, it makes a direct claim upon essence, and therefore aspires toward every version of ultimacy and the absolute' (*SG*, pp. 117–18). This is more sympathetic than 'predatory' or 'imperial', but a degree of distrust persists. We hear the faintest echo of Pope's 'presume not God to scan'.

But for all his distrust of the imperial imagination and of the will-to-power of 'supreme fictions', Donoghue is clearly drawn to the rebellious angels. The most powerful of these angels is Wallace Stevens. Stevens's belief that 'God and the Imagination are one' is, from Donoghue's perspective, both arrogant and subversive, and yet he cannot dismiss Stevens as a poet. Indeed, the adjectives he uses in *The Ordinary Universe* to describe Stevens's poetry convey a fascination that threatens to overwhelm his own scruples: the poetry is 'ravishing' (p. 281), 'vivid' (p. 91), 'handsome' (p. 119), 'dazzling' (p. 228), 'opulent' (p. 282), and 'gorgeous nonsense of the mind' (p. 182). Such adjectives belong to places that are dangerous for the moral self; they make up a 'bower of bliss' that must, with difficulty, be resisted. But they also make the virtues of William Carlos Williams, who does show the proper piety towards things, seem a little dull by comparison. Williams has 'no interest in the kind of thing that interested Stevens: philosophy, ontology, epistemology'; he 'is best understood as a grammarian; skilled in reading the signs'. 'He tried to show what it was like to be alive in a town in New Jersey; not merely the high moments, but the daily feeling of being there' (*OU*, p. 181). Donoghue clearly approves of Williams, but he responds to Stevens with greater emotional intensity.

In the end, Donoghue has to admit that it is not quite enough to be a grammarian of the quotidian. 'If the grammar seems incomplete, the reason is, I suggest, that it lacks a religious dimension' (*OU*, p. 185). Stevens, on the other hand, does have the religious dimension, but it is perceived as heretical: 'The basic motive of *Notes Towards a Supreme Fiction* is to offer man a substitute for God; to show him how he may transfer to himself the attributes and reverberations of the divine' (*OU*, p. 267).

In an earlier study he had put it even more strongly: 'when Stevens ceased to be a Christian he lost all the valid terminologies of action and knew that he could recover them – if at all – only by playing a part in a drama of his own devising. . . . The greatest role he would devise for himself would be God' (*CC*, p. 201). One notes the force of that word 'valid', and one asks 'Valid for whom? Stevens, Donoghue, or the reader?' Personal conviction is here raised to the level of universal absolute; but perhaps this must be true of any criticism that is concerned with values and commitments rather than pure form. Donoghue, at any rate, can be disarmingly frank about his own critical stance. He admits to being 'a little sullen when Stevens subverts' his epistemological position (*OU*, p. 226), and that sullenness surely comes out in the following passage:

> My predicate runs somewhat on these lines. Stevens wrote his poems for a hundred reasons, including this one: to pass the time, to get through the evening. He wrote while waiting: for what? For the maximum disclosure of his own poetic powers. And because this is eight words he often reduced it to one, calling it God: or sometimes to three, calling it the human imagination. Hence and meanwhile there was something to be done. Good or bad, it would be better than its alternative – nothing, the grand zero. (*OU*, p. 228)

This is unfair. Fortunately, it is redeemed somewhat by praise of the late poems, which achieve 'a kind of total grandeur at the end' (*OU*, p. 240). And Donoghue is surely right in saying that Stevens needed, for his best work, an opposing reality, something to be held in tension against his powerful imagination. Such tension reveals the essential 'interdependence of reality and the imagination . . . the wonder of it touches Stevens and excites him to his greatest poetry' (*OU*, p. 276).

In general, however, in *The Ordinary Universe* Williams and Stevens serve as opposite poles in this debate between the claims of reality and those of the imagination. Other poets take part in this debate, but T. S. Eliot is a particularly interesting case. Clearly, he too is at the opposite pole from Williams, although he is treated more kindly than Stevens, presumably because he does not subvert Donoghue's epistemology. In place of the ordinary universe of a town in New Jersey, Eliot offers the vision of the rose-garden, which is 'each man's fantasy-property. In the garden what we hear is not sound, Keats's "heard melodies", but the "unheard music" which is Absolute Sound, since we will settle for nothing less: when we impose our own meaning we are never satisfied by finite gratifications, we lust for the Absolute' (*OU*, p. 245). Eliot's imagination is certainly imperial here; 'impose' gives some recognition of that fact, but the term is less pejorative than, say, 'predatory'. It is significant that he sees Eliot's problem as strategic rather than moral: 'Eliot's problem in *The Four Quartets* is a strategic one; how to evacuate practically all the areas in which his readers live' (*OU*, p. 260). But in the end Eliot's contempt for ordinary things does trouble Donoghue:

> And it points to the deepest embarrassment – or so I think – in Eliot's poetry; the feeling, in part, that all the declared values of human life are somehow illusory and, in part, that nevertheless God so loved the world that He gave up for its redemption His beloved Son. (*OU*, p. 262)

Of the 'three cardinal points of perspective: God, Man, and Nature' (*SG*, p. 26), Eliot denigrates both Man and Nature, while Stevens usurps the role of God and sometimes slights Nature. Ideally, Donoghue would like to see all three terms held in a delicate balance. He came to realize that in *The Ordinary Universe* he had not fully achieved that balance himself: 'In *The Ordinary Universe* I tried to set out a preference for certain writers. . . . But I found myself fending off the versatile giants, trying not to notice their presence' (*TF*, p. 28). These versatile giants are the Prometheans who, like Stevens, impose their vision on the material world. *The Ordinary Universe* was in many respects

a dialogue with Stevens; *Thieves of Fire* is a dialogue with
Eliot in which Donoghue discusses four writers (Milton,
Blake, Melville, and Lawrence) who were 'all, in one degree
or another, alien to T. S. Eliot: he was either indifferent
or hostile to them' (*TF*, p. 19).

Obviously, the term 'Promethean' can imply either praise
or condemnation, depending upon one's point of view.
Donoghue strikes a balance by stressing that the consciousness made possible by the theft of divine fire 'introduces
division into consciousness itself, as a mark of guilt' (*TF*,
p. 25). The consequent 'reflexiveness of mind, which is in
one sense its glory, is in another a token of its criminality,
its transgression at the source' (*TF*, p. 26). Promethean
writers, inheriting this division, cannot simply celebrate
the given world; they must struggle against it, reaching
beyond the limits of the given in an act of primal creative
rebellion; such a struggle is productive of the special fiery
energy that characterizes their work. That energy is marked
by a certain difficulty of style: Milton's style labours under
'the necessity of asserting what once had only to be sung'
(*TF*, p. 46); 'Blake's . . . speech is an act of violence
breaking upon the silence of inertia and habit' (*TF*, p. 66);
in Lawrence's novels 'the language . . . is always straining
beyond itself' (*TF*, p. 111). The struggle at the stylistic
level points to a deeper civil war, so that Milton 'is neither
of the devil's party nor of God's party, but drawn to
division' (*TF*, p. 43), Blake draws his energy from the
contraries of Heaven and Hell, and 'Lawrence was at once
a true Promethean and an acute critic of the Promethean
spirit in himself' (*TF*, p. 127).

It might also be said of Donoghue that, while he may
not be quite of Prometheus's party in that book, neither is
he of Jove's party. Indeed, one may see him, like Milton,
as drawn to the division; he is certainly drawn to the energy
produced by that division, as he makes plain in his book
on Yeats. Yeats 'delights in conflict, because it is a mode
of power'; that 'sense of present power imposes itself,

and the reader finds himself taking everything in that spirit. . . . it is remarkable how persuasive the spirit is and how determinedly Yeats's poems draw an entire life – his own – toward a center of power, whether its official name is passion, energy, will, or imagination' (*WBY*, pp. 4–5). Through the transforming power of the imagination, 'the poet can make himself anew, become his own God, as Nietzsche said' (*WBY*, p. 12). Earlier, Donoghue would have reacted with 'sullenness' to such hubristic claims of the imagination; in that book he can grant Yeats the position that he denied to Stevens, that 'God is the human imagination' (*WBY*, p. 48). It is only when Yeats allows the Nietzschean will to destroy the fine dialectic of consciousness that Donoghue judges him harshly: he complains of 'insistent rhymes' and 'blatancy of rhythm', of a 'shrill tone which I associate with hysteria of the imagination' in some of the last poems (*WBY*, p. 139).

If Nietzsche is responsible for some of the worst stridencies of Yeats's poems, he is also responsible for some of the 'splendor'; he 'propelled Yeats toward the idiom of combat, theater, unity of opposites' (*WBY*, p. 61), and it is this Yeats, who dramatizes his own and the world's conflicts, that Donoghue admires. His finest poetry 'deploys itself in process, along the way of conflict; action incites reaction, statement calls forth counterstatement, each voice is given its due but a rival voice is always heard' (*WBY*, p. 35). The dialogue operates on many levels: between ancient dualities such as good and evil, body and soul, art and nature; between great precursors such as Plato and Blake; and between rival systems: hermetic, gnostic, neo-Platonic. Indeed, as Donoghue suggests, even the organization of the *Collected Poems* is theatrical; each book is 'wrought about a vision, an attitude, a mood', to be followed by 'a new and rival attitude, the mind recoiling from its own creation' in the next book; the pattern is dialectical, and 'we do well to think of the books as personalities in a play' (*WBY*, p. 42).

It is characteristic of Donoghue's own criticism that it too is continually in process, a constant dialogue of the mind with itself over issues of central importance. So, for example, in the mood of *The Ordinary Universe* he was rather hard on symbolism, which he saw as the product of the imperial imagination denying all responsibility toward the realities of daily life, making of the poem 'an object, an icon, a mobile floating free and pure in air' (*OU*, p.128). He saw Yeats as having only the most tenuous connection with symbolism, a passing flirtation from which he was saved by the oral tradition of Irish literature and by his own choice of 'the living world for text' (*OU*, p. 131). But in his book on Yeats, published only three years later, Donoghue recognizes Yeats's version of symbolism as one of the sources of his poetic energy, and redefines the use of symbol. Symbolism, at least as practised by Yeats, is no longer seen as hostile to the world of ordinary things; instead, it 'redeems fact, because through symbol the imagination enters experience, as Christ redeemed fact in the Incarnation (a comparison made, incidentally, in the commentary on Blake by Yeats and Ellis)' (*WBY*, p. 71). The parenthetical attribution of the comparison does not disguise the fact that Donoghue himself has found a way to accept symbolism and the power of the transforming, Promethean imagination by assimilating these forces to his own epistemology. The moment marks a remarkable transformation in his critical stance. Symbol now guarantees 'the presence of the supernatural in the natural'; symbols 'mediate between the individual consciousness, which would otherwise be solipsist, and the given world, which would otherwise be alien' (*WBY*, pp. 71, 72). Piety is no longer to be found solely in the celebratory reverence given to the universe of the quotidian, although it remains essential for the poet to have strong contacts with that universe. Yeats's particular strength is that he admits the symbolist imagination to the test of the realities of time and history; such an 'admission undermines his security as symbolist, but it gives with one hand what it took away with the other; it allows him, by entertaining conflict, to find a more inclusive and a greater art' (*WBY*, p. 83). The journey from Innisfree to Byzantium is taken on 'That dolphin-torn, that gong-tormented sea',[1] itself an image begotten by the Promethean imagination on the brutal facts of mortality.

It might be said, then, that in *Thieves of Fire* and *William Butler Yeats* Donoghue accepts the Promethean imagination as a powerful and productive creative force, one that is not necessarily in conflict with the divine power, and that may in some instances even redeem the world for the word (or the Word). In *The Sovereign Ghost* the redemption of the imagination is carried further, partly because a brute fact in the history of literary criticism has intervened. In his book on Yeats, Donoghue was able to write that 'the single article of faith that goes undisputed in the Babel of modern criticism is the primacy of the creative imagination' (p. 132). But the Babel of modern criticism was soon to lose even that article of faith, and in 'The Essential Power' Donoghue admits that 'imagination is not one of our key terms' (*SG*, p. 1). Not only has it ceased to be a key term, it is heavily under attack. Imagination is inevitably linked to Romantic subjectivity, and the 'privilege of subjectivity is now questioned along with the philosophy of consciousness, the status of the perceiving or speaking subject' (*SG*, p. 38). At one time the imagination was under attack because it placed man, rather than God, at the centre of the universe; indeed, that was the basis of Donoghue's own attack on Stevens in *The Ordinary Universe*. But now the attack comes from structuralists, anthropologists, Marxists, and Freudians, and it is directed not merely against God (long since declared dead), but against the very concept of man as creator, author, autonomous being. Donoghue is now led to ask: 'Is it necessary to revise the standard account of the imagination under pressure from those forces which would displace man from the creative centre of experience and make him rather a function of certain governing systems or codes?' (*SG*, p. 39).

Given this kind of anti-humanist pressure, the imagination becomes 'the essential power'; essential, 'not merely (though this would be cause enough) because it is all we have, but because it is the only force that has the slightest chance of coping with the vast miscellany of arbitrary and ordained events which constitute the occasions of our experience' (*SG*, p. 27). Donoghue begins to sound remarkably like Stevens, the ruefully wise Stevens of 'Final Soliloquy of the Interior Paramour',[2] for whom the imagination is at once pitifully inadequate, 'a single thing, a single shawl / Wrapped tightly round us, since we are poor', and 'a power, the miraculous influence'. In this context the assertion that 'God and the imagination are one' is just that, a desperate assertion, a lone candle to light the dark, and it is made tentatively, almost humbly, without the slightest Romantic swagger. It is important that the statement is prefaced by the limiting 'We say' and that the poem ends on a quiet note of accepted limitation:

> Out of this same light, out of the central mind,
> We make a dwelling in the evening air,
> In which being there together is enough.

I am not suggesting that Donoghue has come round to Stevens's position as a secular humanist. Their positions remain distinct. Stevens lights that candle of the imagination because there is no God; Donoghue makes common cause with him in defending the imagination because, given the intellectual climate of the day, the imagination is the only guarantee (if that is not too strong a word) we have left of our spiritual nature:

Let us say, then, that imagination is the secular name we apply to the soul when we wish to live peacefully with our neighbors. I cannot believe that the imagination is other

than divine in its origin; but even if we leave that belief
aside, or disagree upon it, we may agree that the imagination is a form of energy, demonstrable in its consequences
if not in its nature, and that it strives to realise itself by
living in the world. Like the soul, the imagination seeks to
inhabit not only a human body but a human world. Even
if the given world is regarded as a mere transit camp in a
journey toward the abiding City of God, it is the only world
available to us in the meantime. So a question of the
imagination ranges beyond itself to raise further questions:
the nature of the body, and of "the world's body"; the
character of imagination itself, if such a question is answer-
able; the bearing of imagination as living energy or soul
upon the world it inhabits; and the bearing, gentle or
aggressive, of that world upon its spiritual inhabitant. (*SG*,
p. 29)

I have quoted Donoghue at length here because, as he
himself is aware, the stakes in this project are enormously
high. What he is proposing goes far beyond the boundaries
of literary criticism; it constitutes not only a metaphysics
and politics of the imagination, but, by implication, a
metaphysics and politics of the soul. His opponents are to
be found in two major camps: on the one hand, the rational-
ists (cultural materialists and structuralists of various
persuasions), who would deny the freedom of imagination
(and therefore of soul) and sacrifice the autonomous human
being to a set of structuring forces; on the other hand, the
irrationalists, who would retreat from reason into mind-
lessness and fashionable forms of mystification. The definition of imagination that he proposes, therefore, is analytic
rather than romantic, searching for a possible middle
ground between hostile camps:

I propose therefore to use the word 'imagination' in the
following sense: imagination, as distinct from mind, is that
mental power which finds unnecessary the strict separation
of conscious and unconscious life, of primary and secondary
processes, in Freud's terminology; which deals with contra-

dictions not by subordinating one to another but by accommodating all within a larger perspective; and which enter-
tains feelings and motives before they have been assigned to
categories or organized into thoughts, attitudes, statements,
values, or commitments. (*SG*, pp. 25–6)

The last part of his definition is clearly aimed at those
critics, such as the Marxists, who start from an ideology,
'a theory of relations, and never quite get over the problem
that in studying items and objects they merely seek evidence in their own favour' (*SG*, p. 21). Of course, the
Marxists' reply to Donoghue would be *Et tu quoque*; no
position is ideologically free. Donoghue is aware of this,
and he tries to negotiate a politics of the imagination that
will mediate between romantic subjectivity and historical
necessity. Any 'account of imagination which made it
utterly self-centred, a category of one's private life cut
adrift from questions of natural history, society and culture'
would therefore be unacceptable (*SG*, p. 30). Therefore
it becomes necessary to 'emphasize the intimate relation
between imagination and its enabling correlates: nature,
the world, other people, society, history, the language,
forms, genres' (*SG*, p. 30). Imagination, in other words,
must retreat from the egotistical sublime; it must be contex-
tualized. Having granted critics of romantic subjectivity
such as Adorno their major premise, however, Donoghue
makes clear his acceptance of certain axioms about the
imagination that many structuralists would probably find
both elitist and mystifying:

> that art is the inspired work of a few rare souls, adepts of
> a sacred mystery; that while common minds slide upon the
> surface of things, artists search the depths. The imagination
> cannot believe that what it comes upon or aspires toward
> can be merely contingent, the poet believes that the direc-
> tion of his work is a kind of destiny. (*SG*, p. 32)

His critics would have to admit, however, that at least Donoghue puts his ideological cards on the table.

Moreover, the imagination may be the essential power, but in order for it not to be an imperialistic power it must accept the burden of both time and the ordinary universe. Developing his earlier taxonomy of the imagination, Donoghue now sees it as operating in three modes: the Franciscan, or objective, mode in which 'imagination lavishes attention upon the natural forms' (*SG*, p. 40); the Promethean, or dialectical, mode, in which 'imagination proposes to set against the natural world a rival fiction' (*SG*, p. 41); and the mode of negation, or subjectivism, in which the 'mind repudiates its dependence on objects' (*SG*, p. 43). Of these three modes, according to Donoghue, the structuralists would object only to the second 'because it posits the imagination as creative force, and this would be spurned as romantic mystification' (*SG*, p. 44).

Such statements tend to reduce all the voices in the Babel of modern criticism to one voice; but elsewhere Donoghue does admit that there are differences and that not all structuralists are moral terrorists who would 'represent the speaking subject as dissolved beyond redemption, merely the noise of a ship's wake or a ventriloquist's dummy' (*SG*, p. 61). So, Barthes intends 'only to show the speaking subject as vulnerable to social and political forces' (*SG*, p. 61), and 'Julia Kristeva has argued that we must make a new definition of the transcendental subject so as to allow for its freedom within a social code which the subject at once "rends and renews"' (*SG*, p. 60). The speaking subject, then, is not the autonomous creative self of romantic ideology, but nor is it simply a product of linguistic and social codes; it is constantly caught up in the process of constructing and being constructed. Donoghue can find a meeting place with the structuralists in terms of this process; its tensions and conflicts suggest the continuing possibilities of freedom; 'the code is not yet closed' (*SG*, p. 71). The poet may be born into a system of language, but that 'linguistic code does not remain unmoved as though it were a telephone directory, it registers the force of the poet's mind just as that mind registers the strain involved in wrestling with the language' (*SG*, p. 61).

This tentative accommodation with structuralism allows Donoghue to express a guarded optimism 'that rival positions will not be regarded as a battlefield', and that those, like himself, 'who have an interest in preserving subjectivity and protecting it from the scattering of its properties will be satisfied, so long as their cherished value is not denied' (*SG*, p. 74). But he demands accommodation from the structuralists as well. They must come to terms with 'all the things we cannot help knowing and all the burdens we cannot help feeling'; they must 'reckon with the fact that many of the most powerful codes which govern our lives are contemptible'; and they must beware of replacing 'the old positivism of objects with a new positivism of language' (*SG*, p. 75). In other words, the structuralists must be morally and emotionally responsible. It will be remembered that the same demand was made of the formalists in *The Ordinary Universe*.

The hope expressed at this point for at least a truce with modern critical theory seems to have been premature. At any rate, Donoghue returns to the battle lines in *Ferocious Alphabets*, where he contrasts what he sees as two quite distinct forms of attention that may be given to a text: epireading and graphireading.

> Epireading is not willing to leave written words as it finds them on the page, the reader wants to restore the words to a source, a human situation involving speech, character, personality, and destiny construed as having a personal form. . . . We read a poem not to enlighten ourselves but to verify the axiom of presence: we read to meet the other. The encounter is personal, the experience is satisfying in the degree of presence rather than of knowledge. We read to meet the speaker. (*FA*, p. 99)

In *The Sovereign Ghost* Donoghue had tried to meet the structuralists halfway by adopting some of their terms, such as 'speaking subject'; here he returns defiantly to an old-fashioned terminology that asserts humanistic values. Words such as 'character', 'personality', and 'speaker' are used as a deliberate challenge to contemporary theory, especially as it is embodied by Derrida or Lacan. He seeks to 'verify the axiom of presence' in direct opposition to Derrida's critique of the metaphysics of presence, and he defends the spoken word with all its possibilities of dialogue between living human beings in opposition to Derrida's privileging of the written word. This means that Donoghue is defending the traditions embodied in logocentrism, also under attack by Derrida. These traditions are 'the Christian tradition in which the primal creative principle is identified as the Word of God, God uttering Himself' and 'the metaphysical tradition of the West, which is founded upon the concept of *logos*, the act by which human reason expresses its character' (*FA*, p. 93). It is significant that both Derrida and Donoghue see themselves as speaking against tyranny: for Derrida it is the tyranny of the father, who asserts his power and presence through the act of speaking and who, in Plato's *Phaedrus*, spurns the writing of the son; for Donoghue it is the tyranny of writing, which is seen as 'a dead thing', 'a fixity', in comparison with the dialectical give and take of 'breath and voice' (*FA*, p. 97). Epireading also finds a place for the imagination, since it 'is predicated on the desire to hear; to hear the absent person; to hear oneself in that person' (*FA*, p. 146).

The graphireader, on the other hand, 'deals with writing as such and does not think of it as transcribing an event construed as vocal and audible' (*FA*, p. 151). Donoghue takes as his examples of graphireaders Stéphane Mallarmé, Jacques Derrida, Roland Barthes, Paul de Man, and Lucette Finas, but he could equally well have included those strict formalists who were under attack in *The Ordinary Universe*. The terms of the debate may have changed, but the essential problem of the relation of the text to the world of objects, people, and values remains the same, and Donoghue remains constant through this long debate with himself and others to what might be termed broadly humanistic principles.

In a toughly worded conclusion to *Ferocious Alphabets* he writes:

> Derrida insists that no reconciliation is possible between the humanism of interpretation, voice, presence, discovery and the 'beyond humanism' of play. Each is, in its own way, a ferocious alphabet. If it must come to a choice, I choose the humanism of voice and epireading. (*FA*, p. 206)

He sees Derrida as the 'fanatic of one idea', the maker of an ideology 'the more desperate because it can only suppress what it opposes; or try to suppress it' (*FA*, p. 207).

It might be said that Donoghue himself had worked in *The Ordinary Universe* to suppress what he opposed: the Promethean energy of 'the versatile giants' who challenged his own epistemology. He admits this, as I have already pointed out, with a good grace in *Thieves of Fire*, and he sets about the task of redressing the balance. The dialectical relationship between his own works points to a set of values that transcends what some would regard as his more narrowly held epistemological or theological position: it points to an intellectual honesty that is always willing to examine its own most deeply held beliefs and to a courage and integrity that subjects those beliefs to the challenges of the contemporary intellectual struggle; it points to a delight in process, tension, and conflict as signs of continuing life, energy, and freedom; above all, it points to a profound humanism that is eager to engage in the freedom of discourse, eager to hear, and even to express other voices, not simply for the love of intellectual debate, but because such voices come to us from living, bodily presences in the world, and they demand from us, if we are human, that vital sympathy that we call the imagination.

Pauline Fletcher

In Wallace Stevens's poem 'The Pure Good of Theory', from which the title of this book was taken, 'Time is the hooded enemy':

> It is time that beats in the breast and it is time
> That batters against the mind, silent and proud,
> The mind that knows it is destroyed by time.

'Even breathing is the beating of time', but only 'in kind', and that qualification is enough to yield to time 'a retardation'; out of the temporary fluttering of its murderous pulse arises, 'If we propose', 'a form', 'platonic', unreal but human.

Stevens's poem appears in the introduction to *Ferocious Alphabets*, where it provides a title 'featuring ideological strife among critics'. Donoghue's first lecture in this book continues that concern. Partly indebted to an essay 'The Political Turn in Criticism' (1988), Donoghue's present argument against the unnecessary 'techniques of trouble' of Derrida, Bersani, Jameson, de Man, and Rorty might be aptly summarized by a passage from the earlier piece: 'They compromise the literature they read by subjecting it to a test of good behavior. They defeat the literature in advance. But the question now arises: what form would a serious engagement with literature take, if not a political form which turned it into propaganda?'³

Donoghue's second lecture, entitled 'Towards a Better Life', addresses this question. It deals less with the 'ferocious alphabets' of Stevens's 'destroying spiritual' than with notions, in the broadest sense, of the spiritual itself. In 'The Political Turn in Criticism', Donoghue names these spiritual notions as 'provisional cognition, nominal reason, the production of "consciously false" fictions, imagery of a future consonant with desire, and the antithetical cognitive function which Marcuse called estrangement or contradiction'.⁴ But these are raids on the inarticulate. Here Donoghue circumspectly speaks of such notions as two 'prejudices': the first 'in favour of fictions which offer to tell us not what life is like but what a better life would be like' and the second which claims 'the force of a revelation among the words' (pp. 72–3). But again, Donoghue's rhetoric is equivocal. Initially safeguarded as 'prejudices', then contrarily empowered by 'the force of a revelation', and this further supported by a quotation from Dryden, promising (like Stevens's 'eloquences of light's faculties') revelation in the unverifiable form of light – such prophecies and prejudices lead to questions: Why would the aesthetic imagination propose a better life? Better in what sense?

Donoghue's answer is offered in the concluding section of his second lecture. Indebted to the aesthetic principles of Schiller, who proposed most radically an abandonment of any reference to a validating ontology, Donoghue here reaffirms the intrinsic value of the aesthetic experience. The notion of the intrinsic is dangerous, a state within the state, as Schiller proposed (particularly in his plays) when he reclaimed from the state the interior state of the fine-tuned soul (*feingestimmte Seele*).⁵ Schiller's subversive aesthetic and ethical implications of the fine-tuned soul are summed up in 'the intellectual or moral idea of the intrinsic', which Donoghue reports he first encountered in the notion of the lie in the penny Catechism: ' "No lie can be lawful or innocent; no motive, however good, can excuse a lie, because a lie is always sinful and bad in itself"' (*W*, p. 62). The mysterious quality of the lie, as of the work of art, is the 'in itself'. Neither depends on whether the violated truth is, or even can be, made manifest. Although both the lie and the work of art have infamous representational obligations, art and lies are defined by those only in a functional sense. Donoghue's aesthetics, as he will argue in this volume, leans towards the inward, ethical, or sacramental nature of the intrinsic.

Why the aesthetic has particular qualities one might consider 'better' than those offered by external, historical reality is a question Donoghue asks in *Warrenpoint* (1990) with respect to memory. *Warrenpoint*, Donoghue's autobiography of his boyhood in the town of that name, claims, of course, no such improbable ambitions as Schiller's or Stevens's aesthetic 'form' or Stevens's 'eloquences of light', but it does, I think, aspire to the inward fine-tuned soul. *Warrenpoint* is 'only' a memoir, but memory has in common with art that it provides 'the unofficial sense of history' (*W*, p. 124), and it has in common with the lie that it is not sufficiently defined by its reference and function. That is why *Warrenpoint* is not a remembering of the past but a meditation on remembering. Donoghue's meditations, whether on memory or on art, exemplify the problematic position of the aesthetic imagination between prejudice and revelation, between politics and God.

In *We Irish* (1986) Donoghue admits to an 'occasional inclination to set statesmen right' when politics 'invades literature and prescribes the gross conditions under which poems, plays, stories, and novels are written' (*WI*, p. viii). This is an unusual dramatization. On this side of the Atlantic we are otherwise more accustomed to a disabling absence of 'gross conditions'. The American poet Stanley Kunitz, for one, finds himself 'strangely envious' of 'the

frustrations and anxieties' of Soviet writers (in 1967) who
may risk execution for 'the importance of poetry'.[6]
Responding to the less dramatic, and therefore perhaps
more compromising, conditions of literature in the West,
Donoghue asks in his introduction to *Reading America*
(1987): 'To what extent does our professional interest in
American literature, and our participation in State Department cultural enterprises, commit us to general sympathy
with the aims of an American administration?' One critic[7]
has noted an 'astonishing contradiction' in Donoghue's
answer: 'The easiest way, for a student of American literature, is to keep literature separate from a President's
missionary zeal. I have no gift to set this statesman right.'

Similarly, in a review entitled 'Ire Land',[8] Donoghue
deplores that 'It is pointless to speak of the "problem" of
Northern Ireland if a problem implies a solution. There is
no solution. Instead there is a situation – a situation about
which, as the history of the past 68 years has shown, little
can be done.' The last paragraph of *Warrenpoint* concurs.
The book concludes with a report from the *Irish Times*, for
Thursday, 13 April 1989, of a bombing in Warrenpoint in
which a twenty-year-old woman was killed and thirty-four
people were injured. Here too, Ireland is a situation, not
a problem; little can be done: 'Life in the north goes on,
in some fashion', is how the essay 'Ire Land' closes.

But the last word of *Warrenpoint* is not unequivocal. The
passage records that one of the bombings occurred at the
site of Donoghue's former home: 'The building . . . was
not structurally damaged.' The incident, one senses, is
quoted with resignation; but the site is mentioned with
wonder. About wonder, incidentally, we read in the second
of the present lectures that some part of wonder 'is the
willingness not to draw conclusions from the evidence; or
not to draw them immediately' (p. 76). Memory accomplishes such openings against the closures of history,
and proves, at times, impervious to 'life in time', which
Joseph Campbell has called 'dismemberment'.[9]

Warrenpoint is dedicated to Donoghue's brother, who died at the age of fourteen months. In the impossibility of the address, 'For John, who died', memory arrests dismemberment. It is not, of course, what memory accomplishes, but how it behaves itself on the verge of silence. How can memory 'be other than . . . history?' (*W*, p. 19). How can one reclaim from the state the interior state of the fine-tuned soul, how claim from time 'the eloquences of light's faculties' and imagine, as Stevens writes, 'the speech he cannot speak'?

Such aesthetic and ethical concerns are contrasted to seemingly grander, historic observations when Donoghue admits:

> I wonder about the status of things we forget. According to my family's history, I was brought to the Eucharistic Congress in Dublin in 1932. It was in the summer, in Phoenix Park, and the Pope celebrated Mass, and McCormack sang 'Panis Angelicus', and thousands of people came from all over Ireland to take part in the ceremonies. I have not the least recollection of being present. I was three years and seven months old, and the whole episode is blank to me. But I remember vividly John's death six months later. The first thing I remember was a death in the family. Isn't it strange that I developed – if that is the correct way of putting it – the power of memory just in time to employ it upon the first event worth remembering? (*W*, pp. 30–1)

The question is rhetorical, with a qualifying pause to ponder the 'employment' of memory, and with a sense again of wonder. Donoghue's qualifying 'if that is the correct way of putting it' suspends the conclusion usually drawn from a more deterministic theory claiming that the incisive event initiates the power of memory and the greater power of forgetting and suppression. Perhaps the rhetorical form of the question suspends the answer to the question in what causal relationship memory stands to event, or whether memory might, alas, be held accountable.

The whole passage, with its opening sentence about the status of forgetting, builds towards the problem of remembering, or rather of remembering as a problem. Such moments are frequently pondered throughout the book and contrasted with an abundance of dates, even documentary proof; but the latter suggest only that that is not what is meant, at all. Here memory, ready to 'employ' itself on the death of John, is belated and fails by half a year to record 'the Eucharistic Congress in Dublin', in spite of its attendant splendours. Instead, the 'first event *worth* remembering' (my emphasis) – as if by implication such value were denied the Eucharistic Congress – is John's death, an event noted as an incongruity and with an implicit, if muted, hint of guilt and complaint.

History, so reproachfully charted in the six months between the Eucharistic Congress and John's death and so keenly remembered in the dedication, is irredeemable history, irredeemable because neither the forgetting nor the remembering will affect it. But the charting, the guilt, the reproach, or the regret – or other perhaps more appropriate words of such inward order – constitute an unofficial time, in which loss is entertained in the presence of memory and in which memory attempts, one suspects, some form of redemption of John's brief life.

But these suspicions are secular and unsupported by Donoghue, who holds to the contrary that 'A Christian's conviction impels him to ask, chiefly of his own life: Has it been a valid preparation for the true life to come, when the soul may hope to enjoy the eternal presence of God? The shape is not considered, since life is to be completed only "in our next".' Consequently, few 'possibilities' are ascribed to Donoghue's own life, which takes its dejected beginning 'with the first moment I remember, my brother's death. . . . The site of my possibility coincided with the end of his' (*W*, pp. 127–8). Possibility and impossibility, life and death, beginning and end are here, perhaps without intention, linked by the rhetoric of irony and paradox. But these implicit formal closures are opened to an 'exception': 'The site of my possibility coincided with the end of his; except that we believe, as Catholics, that he is in Heaven' (*W*, p. 128). Human existence is thus not subject to the aesthetic question: 'Had the life a coherent shape, a form, or did it merely break off?' (*W*, p. 127). Nor does Donoghue permit himself the satisfactions of well-wrought forms of memory. Instead, by allowing the interventions of exceptions, memory must serve larger purposes than its own form, larger purposes than the past, and larger purposes than those that can be celebrated by thousands of people from all over Ireland.

Like art, memory is the unofficial historian. Both perform a duty to uphold what Emmanuel Levinas calls ' "an order different from historical time, in which totality is constituted, an order where everything is *pending*, where what is no longer possible historically remains always possible" ' (*W*, p. 124, and 'The Status of Theory', p. 40). Levinas's concept of interiority, which has appeared repeatedly and assumed an important position in Donoghue's more recent work, would hold the promise of envisioning the arrangements of time and events other than by the 'production of the future' (*W*, p. 124) or the logic of causality or the temper of *chronos*. 'Other' would be, as Frank Kermode has aptly put it, to humanize time. Such a time, to which memory seems to give us an immediate and often travelled, if mysterious, access (being the oldest muse), is most severely tested against the formidable argument of John's death. But the test yields the ethical dimensions of humanized time. These dimensions do not diminish or shrink in proportion to temporal distance or factual loss, a thing one feels rather than knows when one of the reviewers of *Warrenpoint* comments: 'Odd this harping on a person (if a fourteen-month-old child can properly be called a person) of whom the memoirist has only the vaguest memories. It is as if this poor, lost mite is here to represent other, greater losses.'[10]

Humanized time echoes Schiller's classical conception of art as our capacity (I paraphrase Schiller) to bring harmony into the variations of our appearance over time and, within the changes of our circumstances, to confirm the absolute and indivisible singularity of personhood.[11] Schiller's word for this capacity is *Formtrieb*, a drive to aesthetic form 'without vulnerable openness to time',[12] 'protected from the battering' as Stevens might say, opposed to 'anything in the world' as Donoghue writes in *The Arts Without Mystery*, 'which completes its meaning elsewhere, apart from its own form' (*AWM*, p. 27).

The intrinsic quality of the work of art provides us with a mental realm 'in which freedom can still be practiced' (*AWM*, p. 125). Donoghue's mildly defensive 'still' nods in the direction of 'a world mostly secular', in which the arts, nevertheless, 'can make a space for our intuition of mystery' (*AWM*, p. 129). That we have such intuitions and that he may speak in universals rather than in historical particulars, Donoghue infers from a larger than historical order, one that passes all understanding but does not arrive at a theology. If even memory might be suspected of having a secret metaphysical assignment in its being other than history, music and sculpture are the most baffling non-mimetic forms of imagination; these forms surpass novels and poems because 'we tend to think they're susceptible to our words: as they are, indeed, but only up to a point' (*AWM*, pp. 142–3). In the present book, Donoghue investigates, with a Jamesian intimation of 'something still deeper', a mystery beyond that point.

It is perhaps impossible not to think of such a mystery in religious terms or to avoid attributing to it religious implications. In *Ferocious Alphabets*, for example, Donoghue suggests that Lucette Finas 'must be a secularist' because her Derridean analysis of a poem by Mallarmé 'deprives the poem of its sacredness, its mystery' (*FA*, p. 195). Donoghue's accusation reminds us of Kierkegaard's critique of those who 'have doubted everything'.[13]

Like Kierkegaard, Donoghue vents his 'misgivings' about premature familiarity, security, or lucidity (*AWM*, pp. 77, 110) or the 'impertinent' assumptions of science and knowledge (*AWM*, p. 132) as if he were denouncing Danish Hegelians who had 'gone further', as Kierkegaard mocks, beyond faith and doubt to the certainties of logic and philosophy. And when pressed hard enough, Donoghue will rail at the 'flabby' discourse of bourgeois humanism with no more than the force of assertion: 'I want discourse to allow for the sense in which the only adequate expression is poetry; and the poetry is adequate only insofar as it beckons beyond itself. I refuse to regard that "beyond" as self-bewilderment or mystification' (*AWM*, pp. 114–15).

Without admitting to having here 'gone further' himself, namely from aesthetics to religion, Donoghue insists that a theory of art cannot be faithful to its task if it succumbs to the omnivorous appetites of secular theory and its imperialist impieties and impatience. 'Beyond' must be preserved as 'beyond', otherness as otherness; the foreignness of the 'foreign lines' of *The Waste Land* is their true meaning (*AWM*, p. 137). Such tantalizing hints of a metaphysics beyond aesthetics have caused at least one critic to remark 'how little Donoghue says about mystery'.[14]

For surely his insistence that what is to be understood is a 'proper form of silence', which is 'the relation between something we say and the misgiving with which we say it, knowing how partial or otherwise inadequate it is' (*AWM*, p. 142) echoes none less than St Paul who reminds us that 'Now we see through a glass darkly . . . now I know in part.' Partial knowledge, in turn, also harbours a mystery: 'Then shall I know even as also I am known' (1 Cor. 13:12). Our 'misgivings' about language thus yearn for revelation, and at certain moments 'language stands baffled' (*AWM*, p. 132). These are, finally, very different notions from those of Barbara Johnson, for example, who argues that 'Literature . . . is the discourse most preoccupied with the unknown, but not in the sense in which such a statement is usually understood. The "unknown" is not what lies beyond the limits of knowledge, some unreachable, sacred, ineffable point toward which we vainly yearn.'[15]

But neither can the metaphysical intimations of Donoghue's aesthetic be reduced to what 'is usually understood'. There are both in this book (pp. 100–1) as well as in *The Arts Without Mystery* (pp. 130–1) clear enough repudiations of the idea that art and religion are in any essential or simple way related. If art, according to Donoghue, permits a sense of freedom from the constraints of time and history, that need not lead to theology, even if it may lead to an ethics. His notion, however, that besides a sense of 'freedom', art also provides a sense of 'presence' (*AWM*, p. 129) remains yet to intimate some revelation.

If 'Writing . . . cannot be present in the sense in which the voice is present to itself within the body' (*FA*, p. 45), literary writing, to borrow a phrase from Gadamer, nevertheless presents not only that which is said, but also itself in the appearing of the reality of its sound (*Es macht nicht nur Gesagtes präsent, sondern auch sich selbst in seiner erscheinenden Klangwirklichkeit*).[16] A literary text thus recovers the lost voice of writing as well as Donoghue's misgivings with which we speak, and requires for Gadamer, not so much a reading as an always 'new, ideal speaking' (*ein neues, ideales Sprechen*). The voice alone can account for the mystery of literary value in that it restores the sensual presence to what Gadamer calls 'the abstraction of writing' (*die Abstraktheit des Geschriebenseins*). Wallace Stevens's 'man lured by a syllable without any meaning' in Stevens's 'Prologues to What Is Possible' is lured 'with an appointed sureness' towards 'a point of central arrival' – that is, a sensual recovery of the silence between words and their meanings.

Donoghue's preference for epireading over graphireading, speech over writing, is hence also a preference for Gadamer's ideal speaking over Derrida's impossibility of speaking, or for Schiller's rather than Derrida's notion of play; for the former is performed in the presence of sound and the indisputable certainties of pleasure, while the latter is performed in the absence of truth and the disputable certainties of knowledge (*FA*, p. 210).

When *Ferocious Alphabets* ends with Donoghue's admission, 'I have no gift to set the philosophers right' (*FA*, p. 209) – we have noted a similar refusal of critical involvement with respect to politics – it should come as no surprise. Although Donoghue engages a number of philosophers/writers on a number of philosophical issues, here, as well as in *Ferocious Alphabets*, his principles of aesthetic judgement derive from and return to no thorny philosophical premise. His aesthetic is based rather on what he calls 'a principle of speech before speech' or 'the aboriginal situation' (*FA*, p. 151), one that would reflect Levinas's priority of 'man's ethical relation to the other' over 'his ontological relation to himself'.[17] With such a principle, finally, one might have arrived at 'something still deeper' than the referential obligations of words and their always deferred promises.

In an insightful essay,[18] Donoghue suggests that Irving Feldman's poem 'The Flight from the City' closes with the notion of an aboriginal situation, a situation which Feldman, significantly, represents by a scream. Donoghue points out: 'The scream is authentic. It is not, like Munch's painted screams or Francis Bacon's the scream of one's own being, in anguish and yet in self-regard. It is for another, for the sake of another's soul.' Donoghue's word 'authentic' is highest praise. It implies that the primordial situation is communal, although a scream has neither grammar nor syntax nor beauty; it is uttered without will or intention, and yet it has meaning by virtue of the voice alone.

James's notion of 'something deeper' attributed to Maisie's knowledge is revealed by 'a short jerk' of her arms. Like the scream, it is an unwilled but indisputably meaningful gesture in itself. Responding to J. Hillis Miller's reading of the same passage in his *Versions of Pygmalion* (1990), Donoghue argues here that any meaning of Maisie's jerk is available only to a sympathetic suspension of the will to purpose and knowledge – that is, 'to perception alone' (p. 82). But such a purposeless perception may want to bear too little or too much reality: too little if the perception is to suggest that it is only a work of art we are perceiving and not the unknown before which it stands baffled and beyond which it beckons; and too much if it is Dionysos himself who calls for Miller's Apollonian desire to 'evaluate', 'admire', or 'emulate'. Whether as a pure aesthetic or as an 'ethical *casus*' (p. 82), both Donoghue's and Miller's responses are forms of interpretive domestication, both omnivorously so, both fearing a silence in which something beyond intelligence, as Stevens would say, might yet be heard – or, more terrible, might not be heard. The scream is uttered in a similar terror of silence. If for Miller the silence would resound with the disappearance of God, Donoghue might insist otherwise.

Harold Schweizer

REFERENCES

The following works by Denis Donoghue are cited in the Introduction:
Connoisseurs of Chaos (1965) (*CC*)
The Ordinary Universe (1968) (*OU*)
William Butler Yeats (1971) (*WBY*)
Thieves of Fire (1974) (*TF*)
The Sovereign Ghost (1976) (*SG*)
Ferocious Alphabets (1981) (*FA*)
The Arts without Mystery (1983) (*AWM*)
We Irish (1986) (*WI*)
Warrenpoint (1990) (*W*)

NOTES

1   *The Collected Poems of W. B. Yeats* (London: Macmillan, 1961), p. 281.
2   *The Collected Poems of Wallace Stevens* (New York: Knopf, 1987). Subsequent quotations are from this edition.
3   Denis Donoghue, 'The Political Turn in Criticism', *Salmagundi* 81 (Winter 1988), pp. 111–12.
4   Ibid., p. 116.
5   *Schillers Werke*, vol. 10, *Über die ästhetische Erziehung des Menschen*, siebenundzwanzigster Brief (Basel: Birkhäuser, 1968), p. 207.
6   Stanley Kunitz, 'A Visit to Russia', in *A Kind of Order, A Kind of Folly* (Boston: Little, Brown, 1975), p. 18.
7   Bruce Bawer, 'Reading Denis Donoghue', *The New Criterion*, October 1987, p. 30.
8   Denis Donoghue, 'Ire Land', *New Republic* 201, no. 25, (18 December 1989), p. 38.
9   Joseph Campbell, *The Hero with a Thousand Faces* (Princeton: Princeton University Press, 1948; repr. 1968), p. 25.
10 John Banville, 'Portrait of the Critic as A Young Man', *New York Review of Books*, (15 October 1990), p. 48.
11 The relevant passage reads as follows: 'Der zweite jener Triebe, den man den Formtrieb nennen kann, geht aus von dem absoluten Dasein des Menschen oder von seiner vernünftigen Natur und ist bestrebt, ihn in Freiheit zu setzen, Harmonie in die Verschiedenheit seines Erscheinens zu setzen und bei allem Wechsel des Zustands seine Person zu behaupten. Da nun die letztere als absolut unteilbare Einheit mit sich selbst nie im Widerspruch sein kann . . . umfasst [der Formtrieb] mithin die ganze Folge der Zeit' (*Schillers Werke*, vol. 10, pp. 122–3).
12 Ibid., p. 140.
13 Søren Kierkegaard, *Fear and Trembling*, tr. Hong and Hong (Princeton: Princeton University Press, 1983), p. 5.
14 Eugene E. Selk, 'Review of *The Arts without Mystery*', *Journal of Aesthetics and Art Criticism* 43 (1985), p. 414.
15 Barbara Johnson, *The Critical Difference: Essays in the Con-*

temporary Rhetoric of Reading (Baltimore: Johns Hopkins University Press, 1980), p. xii.

16 Hans-Georg Gadamer, *Wahrheit und Methode: Grundzüge einer philosophischen Hermeneutik*, vol. 1 (1960; repr. Tübingen: J. C. B. Mohr, 1986), and *Ergänzungen/Register*, vol. 2 (1986), p. 352.

17 'Dialogue with Emmanuel Levinas' (Emmanuel Levinas and Richard Kearney), in *Face to Face with Levinas*, ed. Richard A. Cohen (Albany: State University of New York Press, 1986), p. 21.

18 Denis Donoghue, 'Notes on "The Flight from the City"', in *Irving Feldman's Poetry: Nine Essays*, ed. Harold Schweizer (Lewisburg: Bucknell University Press, 1992), p. 181.

The Status of Theory

On 16 January 1956, R. P. Blackmur gave a lecture at the Library of Congress under the title 'The Techniques of Trouble', second in the series of his four lectures later published as *Anni Mirabiles 1921–1925: Reason in the Madness of Letters*, a meditation on modern literature and the conditions, mostly terrible, that made the literature possible. One of those conditions was that the new forms of knowledge had come out as techniques 'for finding trouble in ourselves and in the world'. It was almost, Blackmur said, 'as if to make trouble had become the creative habit of the general mind'. The new forms of knowledge he named were psychology, 'which dissolved the personality into bad behaviour'; anthropology, which dissolved religion into a competition of monsters; psychiatry, which cured the disease by making a monument of it; and sociology, which flattened us into the average of the lonely crowd. In life, Blackmur maintained, 'we do what we can and what we must'; in literature and the arts (and sometimes in our daydreams and what we call our thought) 'we make a kind of rival creation always, one way or another, in response to the actual life itself'; and in our great creations 'we alter that actual life in the sense that we alter what we think about it, what we acknowledge about it, what we see in it, and what we do about it in our private selves where most of our time is spent'.[1]

I have recalled that episode, Blackmur's lecture, mainly

to say that theory, whatever in addition it may be, is another technique of trouble, a device to make trouble for ourselves. But I want to hold open the question of rebuke to allow for the fact that some forms of trouble are worth making, and some trouble-makers are later seen to have worked for the common good. If the new knowledges seemed to Blackmur to undermine personality, conviction, belief, and human relations, theory seems to me to continue the work of trouble by other means. So we have scepticism in the guise of philosophy, suspicion and resentment as hermeneutics, unanswerable questions in the scene of reading. So why do I persist in thinking that making trouble is not – or not necessarly – the same as making a nuisance?

It is hard to say when the trouble-making began. It didn't begin in 1967 when Jacques Derrida published *De la grammatologie*. It would be just as reasonable to say that it began with Plato's dialogues; but saying that would release us from the immediate need to pay attention. If Plato's questions in the *Phaedrus* and the *Protagoras* haven't yet been answered, they can wait a little longer. Perhaps it would be better to settle upon a certain historical moment when, as it seems to me, the conditions for a certain style of discourse emerged. I don't say that they emerged then for the first time, but that they were the particular conditions we recognize as prefiguring our own.

Let us begin, as so much of moment to us begins, with Matthew Arnold; specifically with his determination, in *Literature and Dogma* as in *Culture and Anarchy*, to suspend his reliance upon the facts of creation as Christianity adduced them, and to trust rather in the emotions that accompanied their production. Arnold persuaded himself that he could let the truths of Christianity go, disabled by science as they seemed to be, and hold on to the emotions that had long attended them. If he could retain the emotions and find them expressed in the masterpieces of literature and drama, he could, he thought, sustain his spiritual life. He would have nothing to say of first-and-last things, but he hoped none the less that he could discuss serious public and private issues. He would no longer recite the doctrines of Christianity or discuss with philosophers the arduous nicety of *logos*, being, and knowledge, but he might still present in secular terms the issues he regarded as crucial. These were bound to be social and political issues and to bear upon questions of education. They were also bound to retain something of the religious weight and force which Arnold had apparently discarded. We may think of them as a 'translation downward' of fundamental religious questions which Arnold was not now in a position to address in doctrinal terms. So it is not quite accurate to say that his themes and terms were secular; they were secular, indeed, but they remembered their origin in religion and conducted themselves with a certain misgiving.

Culture and Anarchy is a choice example of what we call 'critical theory' or 'culture criticism'. It is not literary theory or literary criticism, if only because its relation to literature is occasional and opportunistic. Arnold's interest in literature is not, as we used to say, an intrinsic interest; he is not interested in poems as exhibiting the play of language and mind. For him, literature is always exemplary and illustrative. When he quotes a phrase or a few lines, it is because he wants to illustrate a particular sentiment or a certain style or tone he thinks important for society at large. As in *On Translating Homer* and *On the Study of Celtic Literature*, there are certain tones of feeling in literature which he wishes to propagate in the manners of English society. A style in literature corresponds to a possible way of life. Now that he has given up the right to use the terms of Christianity or to avail himself of its morality, Arnold must make do with the ordinary terms at hand. It is a mark of his skill in rhetoric that he can so use commonplace words as to make them do the work of a more technical vocabulary. He invokes his favourite phrases so often – 'sweetness and light', 'our best self', 'an inward working', 'the main current of human life' – that it requires an effort of detachment on our part to realize that these phrases mean only as much or as little as we agree to let them mean; they have no force in themselves, apart from our goodwill. If we once ask ourselves what exactly 'sweetness' means or 'light' means, Arnold's sentences lose their power over us; we become immune to them.

It was Arnold, none the less, who devised a style in which nearly anything, short of the ultimate questions of life and death, could be offered for common discussion. The great Victorian controversies required such a style, and were conducted in it with parliamentary verve and flourish. As a strictly literary critic, Arnold was not at his best. He never wrote anything, in that way, comparable to Henry James's prefaces to the New York edition of his novels. But as a campaigner, satirist, and polemicist, Arnold was supreme, and he made available to later generations a public style in which nearly anything could be said that had to be said. It was Arnold's style, even more than his local argument, that persuaded I. A. Richards of the possibility of conducting an intelligible life without belief or beyond belief. At least in his early books, Richards thought that he could discuss the main issues of language, meaning, interpretation, aesthetics, and psychology by bringing together the deliverances of science and poetry; science for the broad truth of things, poetry for the fine adjustment of impulses and forms.

Indeed, critical theory in the English language might have continued to flourish in the spirit of Arnold and of Richards if a new and revolutionary literature had not proved itself opaque to such attention. Nothing in Arnold's common style, or even in Richards's, was prepared for the apprehension of *Ulysses*, *The Waste Land*, and Pound's early *Cantos*. It was clear that these works, to be read at all, required the closest attention to surface and structure. The New Criticism, as it emerged in the early writings of Eliot and then of Richards, Empson, Leavis, Ransom, Burke, Blackmur, Tate, and their colleagues, was a method of reading, provoked by the new poetry and fiction. That it was also in opposition to certain conventions of scholarship, literary history, the history of ideas, and other procedures in graduate schools made the provocation opportune. It is true that the pedagogical programme was still, according to Arnold, to make students hospitable to the best that had been thought and said in the world. The addition of new poems and novels to the curriculum did not undermine the spiritual value of the tradition; indeed, it extended its force. But Arnold's style was not sufficiently analytic to enable readers to take possession of the new works by Eliot, Pound, Joyce, and Yeats. Criticism continued to be written in a fairly understandable style, but Eliot's definition of wit, Cleanth Brooks's dealing with irony, Empson's with ambiguity, Kenneth Burke's with progression, and Blackmur's wooings of the sublime pointed the reader toward more strenuous engagements with verbal detail than anything promised or threatened by Arnold.

These critics did not think of themselves as theorists. They were looking for principles, or trying to turn their prejudices into images and axioms. The principles, in Burke, Empson, Brooks, Warren, and Tate, were mainly political; a politics of the Left in Burke and Empson, of the Right in the others. The principles Richards sought had to meet the requirements of science, especially neurology and psychology. Eliot's principles were religious and eventually doctrinal, Ransom's were aesthetic and philosophical. In every case, they were principles rather than theories. The difference, I take it, is that a theory is a set of considerations established ahead of time and as justification of the values in the case. In that sense John Rawls wrote *A Theory of Justice* to say what the concept of justice might be thought to be. Principles are a set of considerations, in regard to a value already established, which will be judged in their practical applications; as we sustain principles of justice by acting in the light of them. When Richards wrote *Principles of Literary Criticism*, he had in view that readers would put his principles into practice and thereby become better readers. He was not concerned with the formulation of a theory of literature, but rather to improve the practice of something already there and widely, if badly, practised: literary criticism.

It is clear that the common search for principles, in that understanding of them, has largely been abandoned; or, if not abandoned, handed over to experts in particular areas of inquiry – ethics, morals, law, and political science. It is rare to find ethical or moral principles adduced in any supposed bearing upon the practice of reading works of literature. J. Hillis Miller, Laurence Lockridge, and other critics are engaged in a different effort. Perhaps we consider that a relation between ethical or moral principles and the reading of a work of literature is bound to be a crude affair if the only question that arises is whether the principles are acknowledged or ignored. We might also think that we have done well to abandon the question of principles and instead to pursue a feasible theory of whatever it is we want to establish. We might claim that we had given up our prejudices and elected to move among considerations speculative and experimental. It could be argued that literature, which is largely and perhaps entirely fictive, should be prefigured by notions and hypotheses, the work of speculative instruments. If we can't say anything about first-and-last things, and if scientists tell us that the best part of their work is hypothetical and notional, then it would seem reasonable to pursue our theories in a mood hospitable and airy.

But we soon discover that our discourses are not at all hospitable. On the contrary: we find that the favoured terms of reference and agency are far more likely to threaten than to invite. If the word 'theory' denotes a loose federation among scholars of diverse interests, and if many of these share nothing but a prejudice that they have certain enemies in common, then it is strange that the play supposedly of notions and hypotheses, by definition severed from the ultimate questions, is conducted in remarkably insistent terms. Reading essays in critical theory, I often find myself wondering about the authors: where have they found such conviction, in the declared absence of any ground of ultimacy? They tell me that nothing can be established, but they show no misgiving in producing a tone of certitude in the admonition. Having rid themselves and us of certainty, they seem unwilling to act upon the diminished thing or to learn a tentative style from a despair. It begins to appear that theory denotes not an affiliation of theorists in search of tenable theories to establish whatever it is that exerts a claim upon them; but, on the contrary, a concatenation of largely independent ideologies as blatant as the certitudes they begin by undermining.

I propose to refer to three or four fairly recent occasions in the rhetoric of theory and to ask whether we can make peace, if not common cause, with their proponents. I begin with a long section of Derrida's *La Vérité en peinture*, devoted to Kant's third Critique. Now Derrida has told us that deconstruction is not a theory; indeed, that it resists theory because it 'demonstrates the impossibility of closure, of the closure of an ensemble or totality on an organized network of theorems, laws, rules, methods'.[2] It is not a theory, a method, or a system. In reading its texts, deconstruction is not concerned with discursive contents, themes, or theses, but rather with 'institutional structures'. Presumably these are the socially accredited axioms, so far as they are empowered as such, which make possible certain verbal practices. Deconstruction has an aim but not a method; its aims are to detect the working of pervasive but invisible axioms and, by disclosing them, to remove the privilege and the authority they have contrived to give to the texts at hand. In *La Vérité en peinture*, for instance, Derrida examines Kant's account of adherent beauty and free beauty – *pulchritudo adhaerens* and *pulchritudo vaga* – and claims that it 'depends in an essential manner . . . on a pragmatic anthropology and on what would be called, in

more than one sense, a reflexive humanism'. This anthropological humanism, Derrida maintains, 'weighs massively,
by its content, on this supposedly pure deduction of aesthetic judgement'.[3] By 'anthropological' Derrida means
that Kant's instances are for man, in the service of man;
that man is the final goal of nature.

The question before us is not: Is Derrida right or wrong
about Kant? or even, has he indeed detected the axiom,
the prejudice, that supposedly sustains Kant's account of
aesthetic judgement? He implies that Kant's account is
caught red-handed, caught out, and that the culprit is a
pragmatic anthropology, otherwise known as a reflexive
humanism. The implication is that we should construe
everything that Kant says in the third Critique as a consequence of his humanism, and therefore explain it perhaps
to the extent of explaining it away. But if there is no such
thing as a presuppositionless statement – as I'm content to
believe – I can't see that Kant is in any worse position than
Derrida is, or myself. If Kant defines an *a priori* judgement
as one that is independent of experience, not derived from
experience but from imperatives of universality and necessity, it is trivial to remark that his definition depends, in
turn, upon whatever he means by universality and by
necessity. I don't at all disagree with Derrida's commentary
so far as the detail goes, but only with his implication that
he has caught Kant out in a piece of self-deception. It
would indeed be reprehensible if Derrida were to take it
for granted that a discourse issuing from a self-reflexive
humanism is self-evidently tainted by that origin; but he
doesn't go so far. If he did, it would be necessary to detect
his own particular prejudice at work.

I hope to show, in two or three further instances, how
the work of theory – which sounds as if it were, or ought
to be, speculative, notional, and experimental – is, more
often than not, blatantly tendentious. Leo Bersani has
recently published an essay called 'Against *Ulysses*'. His
argument is that Joyce's novel is not what it pretends or

claims to be: a challenging, interrogative work of modernism. On the contrary, Bersani says, it is a nineteenth-century realistic novel of character and personality, predicated upon 'a conservative ideology of the self'. The implication of the book is that in Joyce's mind, at last, not only has nature become culture but culture has become man. 'Joyce is faithful to our humanist tradition', Bersani says, 'in his reenactment of its assumptions and promise that the possession of culture will transcend anxiety and perhaps even redeem history'. He 'gives us back our culture as *his* culture'. Finally, *Ulysses* domesticates the forces with which it deals, and shows us the form a serene possession of cultural constituents would take. *Ulysses* is not, then, a great *avant-garde* work. The contrast to be made in that respect is between Joyce and Beckett:

> (Sociability in Joyce is a function of realistically portrayed characters, and not, as in Beckett, the fascinatingly anachronistic remnant of the disappearance of such characters.) Beckett's authentic avant-gardism consists in a break not only with the myths fostered by cultural discourse, but more radically, with cultural discourse itself. The mystery of his work is how it is not only sustained but even begun, for intertextuality in Beckett (the echoes of Descartes and of Malebranche in the early works, for example) is not a principle of cultural continuity (as it is in Joyce, in spite of the parodic nature of the repetitions), but the occasion for a kind of psychotic raving. . . . [In Joyce] the parodistic replays of Homer, Shakespeare, and Flaubert – not to speak of all the authors 'quoted' in 'Oxen of the Sun' – are neither subversive of nor indifferent to the fact of cultural inheritance; rather, Joyce relocates the items of that inheritance with *Ulysses* as both their center and belated origin.[4]

Bersani is dismayed to find that *Ulysses* permits us to think of its characters as if they existed before the beginning of the book and might be deemed to continue after the last page. Even a reader as subtle as William Empson specu-

lated that the first thing Molly Bloom will do with Stephen
Dedalus is make him take a bath. But Bersani's dismay is
an old story. Many years ago L. C. Knights wrote an essay
called 'How Many Children Had Lady Macbeth?', the title
a parody of critical concern with questions of character. In
those days F. R. Leavis, Knights, and other critics argued
that Shakespeare's plays are not novels of character but
dramatic poems most completely disclosed in structures of
imagery. Bersani's complaining reference to a conservative
ideology of the self has in view not only the fact that Joyce
allows us to imagine that his characters exist, but that we
are encouraged to believe that their existence is a function
of the internal lives ascribed to them. We believe in the
existence of Leopold Bloom because we find that he has
full access to a distinctive internal life. Or so it appears.
My own sense of the matter is that our assent to Leopold
Bloom is not a matter of belief but of supposition; if he
were to exist, he would indeed have these thoughts and
ramblings. We proceed as if he existed, while knowing
that he doesn't. But Bersani writes, in this essay, as if a
conservative ideology of the self were automatically to be
judged foolish or wicked. He has not done anything to
establish such a judgement. Indeed, if he resents the plenitude of the inner lives ascribed to Leopold Bloom, Stephen,
Molly, and many other characters in the book, I can't see
how he is entitled to his resentment. Surely Levinas is
right to say, as he does in *Totality and Infinity*, that 'the
inner life is the unique *way* for the real to exist as a
plurality', and again that 'interiority is the very possibility
of a birth and a death that do not derive their meaning
from history'. Interiority 'constitutes an order different
from historical time, in which totality is constituted, an
order where everything is *pending*, where what is no longer
possible historically remains always possible'.[5]

Bersani's objections to *Ulysses* would be equally appli-
cable to any realistic novel. He seems to resent the fact

that the novel that was supposed to bring realism to an end did not do so, and that Joyce may not have intended to bring realism to an end. Indeed, I would maintain that in *Ulysses* Joyce uses so many conventions of fiction, including realism, that it is hard to suppose he wanted to render any of them null. The fact that many of the most serious novelists are writing realistic novels can hardly be found scandalous. We are living at a time when writers may do as they please, may subscribe to any convention that appeals to them. It would be wicked to try to thwart them, out of respect for some notion of literary history which they, more often than not, disregard. Bersani associates realism with a conservative ideology of the self, and resents the association. But his objection to this ideology is merely an objection like any other; it conveys a prejudice like any other. If he were to dislike a radical or subversive ideology of the self, his sentiment would still be merely that, a prejudice equal and opposite.

Ulysses has also been an occasion of scandal to Fredric Jameson, for similar and for different reasons. Jameson has long resented the particular version of modernism which he associates with Joyce and Eliot on the grounds that in such works as 'The Love Song of J. Alfred Prufrock', *A Portrait of the Artist as a Young Man*, and *Ulysses*, these writers make available certain devices for converting an alienated world into personal styles and modes of inwardness. In one respect, Jameson's attack on Eliot and Joyce is the standard Marxist attack on the subjective emphasis in modern literature. Lukács and other critics argued that many works of modern literature present individual characters as lonely, isolated figures and then endow that loneliness with a metaphysical *aura*, the glamour of their doom. In the 'Circe' chapter of *Ulysses*, as Jameson reads it, the details are 'unified by the stylistic *tone* in which all contradictions are ironically resolved as well as by the overall unity of Mr. Bloom's personality'.[6] Joyce, that is to say, keeps faith with the illusions of subjectivity. Meanwhile the social conditions at large remain unchanged; there is no impulse to go out and change them.

In a later essay called '*Ulysses* in History', Jameson develops these points into an attack not only on that novel, but on the entire tradition of symbolism in which it is allegedly implicated. He starts by referring to 'the modern' or 'modernity' as involving a crisis, 'something like a dissociation between meaning and existence'. Jameson's authority for this is Roland Barthes, whom he quotes on 'the great mythic opposition between the *vécu* – the lived experience – and the intelligible'. Jameson then extends the alleged opposition between the lived experience and the intelligible into an attack on symbolism. Symbolism involves, he says, 'the illicit transformation of existing things into so many visible or tangible meanings'.[7] Jameson has in mind that if nature has now been transformed into culture, and if cultural events and artifacts are still felt as degraded, then it is absurd to endow any of them with an *aura* of significance.

This argument of Jameson's may remind you of another version of it, Paul de Man's in *Blindness and Insight*, where de Man refers to the contradictory relations between natural 'Being and the consciousness of Being'.[8] Romanticism is the phase or mode of literature in which writers try either to resolve the contradiction or to live with it. The romantic symbol has long been understood as the sign of a possible, if intermittent and unforeseeable reconciliation between man and nature, the being of consciousness and natural being. Wordsworth's 'spots of time' are moments in which the feeling of discrepancy between him and the world in which he finds himself is somehow alleviated. Paul de Man had an interest in showing that such moments of a felt harmony are delusions, and that the most honourable figure of thought is not symbol but allegory, because allegory always testifies to the gap between experience and meaning:

Whereas the symbol postulates the possibility of an identity
or identification, allegory designates primarily a distance in
relation to its own origin, and, renouncing the nostalgia
and the desire to coincide, it establishes its language in the
void of this temporal difference. In so doing, it prevents
the self from an illusory identification with the non-self,
which is now fully, though painfully, recognised as a non-
self.[9]

It seems to me that de Man, Jameson, and Barthes
are making unnecessary trouble; they are setting up an
exorbitant demand and taking grim pleasure in claiming
that it can't be satisfied. The relation between lived experience and intelligibility is not – or not necessarily – one of
contradiction. Whose experience is it anyway? I can't
believe that Barthes thought his experience unintelligible;
his essays and books are remarkable precisely for the skill
with which he discerned intelligible forms and patterns
where one would least expect to find them. Am I to believe
that Jameson finds his experience unintelligible? If he does,
he speaks from it with remarkable conviction. As for Paul
de Man, what is his evidence for referring to the contradictory relations between natural being and the being of consciousness? Where is the contradiction? Difference there
is, in the sense that the mode of being of a stone is not the
same as the mode of being of a mind; but there is no
contradiction unless I demand that the two modes should
be the same and discover that they're not. De Man is doing
a number of things which he is under no obligation to do.
First, he describes a certain desire, without calling it by
its proper name, an extreme form of idealism: it is the
desire to identify being with knowledge and knowledge
with the subjection of the multiplicity of reality to the
unifying insistence of one's mind. Second, he implies that
this desire is universal; third, that its corresponding figure
is the symbol; fourth, that the gratification of symbolic
knowledge is spurious; fifth, that allegory is more honour-

able than symbolism because it incorporates the sad conviction that symbolic knowledge is an illusion. None of these
five steps is obligatory. Levinas is again entirely right in
saying, as he does in an essay on Proust, that Proust's most
profound vision consists in 'situating reality in a relation
with something that forever remains other, with the Other
as absence and mystery', and in 'rediscovering this relation
in the very intimacy of the "I"'.[10] The simple point is
that allegory and symbolism are two figurative procedures,
corresponding to two different but not contradictory
moods.

The last example of a 'technique of trouble' which I
propose to comment on may appear an eccentric choice
because it seems to provide a method of avoiding trouble.
It is a recent essay by Richard Rorty called 'Foucault/
Dewey/Nietzsche'. The essay is mainly about Foucault,
whom Rorty sees as 'a Romantic intellectual' split between
two loyalties. The first of these may be called Foucault's
citizenship, his desire to join with his fellow-citizens of a
democracy in trying to improve the conditions at large and
make life better for everyone. The second is loyalty to
himself, or to a private vision of himself: it involved 'his
private search for autonomy, his refusal to be exhaustively
describable in words which apply to anyone other than
himself'. Rorty believes that intellectuals should keep these
two loyalties separate; should live two lives, public and
private, the life of a citizen and the life of a seer, a visionary.
Intellectuals should be free, Rorty maintains, to pursue
their autonomy in private, free to think inhuman thoughts,
but should never try to impose these private visions on
anyone else:

> Just as Kierkegaard's knight of faith looks like a bank clerk,
> and in public acts like one, so the Romantic intellectual can
> be, for public purposes, your ordinary bourgeois liberal. It
> is only when a Romantic intellectual begins to want his
> private self to serve as a model for other human beings that

his politics tends to become antiliberal. When he begins to think that other human beings have a moral duty to achieve the same inner autonomy as he himself has achieved, then he begins to think about political and social changes which will help them do so. Then he may begin to think that he has a moral duty to bring about these changes, whether his fellow citizens want them or not.[11]

Now at first sight Rorty seems to be offering an attractive programme. If it were to be followed, Jameson would keep his Marxism to himself, de Man would pursue his scepticism in his private time, and Bersani would refine his radical ideology of the self and would not disturb the neighbours by publishing it. I, in turn, would keep my religious beliefs to myself, so far as they differ – as apparently they do – from the values which for Rorty constitute citizenship. Rorty is clear about these. Indeed, he is so sure of them that he removes them from discussion; without any ado, he refers to 'we liberals in the U.S.A.', again to 'we liberal reformists', to 'a good humanitarian bourgeois liberal', and to 'societies, at their liberal, social-democratic best'. Rorty takes bourgeois liberalism for granted, and ignores the consideration that bourgeois liberalism is merely one ideological position among many. He provides not one word of reasoning in its favour, but speaks of it as if it issued spontaneously and irrefutably from the nature of things.

I should perhaps assure you that, in practice, my attitude to bourgeois liberalism is just as warm as Rorty's. But I am not prepared to identify it with citizenship quite as unquestioningly as he is. I note, too, that while Rorty refers to 'we liberal reformists', he does not indicate any of the reforms he advocates. He seems content to leave social conditions, at least in the United States, exactly as they are. Or at least, he doesn't suggest that any of them should be changed. In the essay in question, Rorty is conducting an exercise in ideology, and is proceeding as if his ideological position were beyond question. He writes on the understanding that the claims of citizenship are supreme, that the system of values which fulfils the definition of citizenship is that of bourgeois liberalism, and that anyone's private or further definition of his or her self must be in a relation, however antithetical, to bourgeois liberalism. But if I were to tell Rorty that as a Christian I regard my true citizenship – the one for which I live in hope – as that of the city of God, and that I regard my citizenship of a certain democratic state as secondary and contingent, I can't see how the conversation could continue. Rorty assumes that the only feasible discourse is political, and that among the possible political systems one of them, bourgeois liberalism, is self-evidently the only right one.

At this point you may be reminded of a certain moment in the history of modern poetry. In the Spring 1938 issue of *The Yale Review* Archibald MacLeish wrote an essay on Yeats's poetry in which he quoted Thomas Mann as saying that 'In our time the destiny of man presents its meaning in political terms'. When Yeats read the essay, he wrote a poem called 'Politics', and prefaced it with the quotation from Mann. The poem then runs:

> How can I, that girl standing there,
> My attention fix
> On Roman or on Russian
> Or on Spanish politics?
> Yet here's a travelled man that knows
> What he talks about,
> And there's a politician
> That has read and thought,
> And maybe what they say is true
> Of war and war's alarms,
> But O that I were young again
> And held her in my arms![12]

If the poem were accompanied by a discursive argument,

it might go somewhat on these lines. Every vocabulary, once chosen and settled upon, develops a totalizing ambition: it tries to round itself out and to appropriate the whole space of the world. It is not content to speak in local terms of partial situations; it wants to displace every other vocabulary and to declare its own vision a comprehensive one. A political vocabulary is ambitious to this degree. Yeats might say in reply to Mann that the vocabulary of sex has an ambition equal and opposite to that of politics, and that its claim upon one's passion is at least as resolute. Alasdair MacIntyre has argued, in *After Virtue*, that the reason why the public debate of moral and ethical issues is interminable is that the various concepts which inform our moral discourse are merely fragments broken off from discourses that were once comprehensive but are now in ruins; they were originally 'at home in larger totalities of theory and practice in which they enjoyed a role and function supplied by contexts of which they have now been deprived'.[13] I would add another reason: that the totalizing zeal of a vocabulary – of any and every vocabulary, indeed – expresses itself not only by capturing the entire space but by excluding those people who do not speak that particular idiolect. So we recognize an ideology by the words it uses, the phrases it habitually resorts to, and the refusal to use the words of any other ideology.

It begins to appear – as it has appeared to me for some time – that far from being beset with theory, or with the techniques of trouble which go under that name, what we encounter is not theory at all; it is merely a number of ideologies going about their business. I do not intend an insult when I call these forms of business paper wars; we are all engaged in them.

I hope you understand that I am not, in the vulgar phrase, 'against theory'. Not to have a theory is to be enslaved to someone else's. What I am against is the confusion of theory with principle – or rather, the confusion of theories with principles and ideologies – and the prosecution of principles and ideologies under the pseudonym of theory. Indeed, I wish we had in our profession several forms of discourse meriting the name of theory, and in that spirit I have a suggestion to make. It may be made by referring to an apparently innocuous occasion in the rhetoric of philosophy.

Ralph Barton Perry was chairman of the Department of Philosophy at Harvard from 1906 to 1913. He was not, I suppose, an original thinker, but he had a clear mind and he explained things lucidly. Much of his work arose from consideration of certain ideologies: naturalism, idealism, pragmatism, and realism. His most telling essays issued from debates with Royce and William James. His best book is *The Thought and Character of William James* (1935). In a lesser book called *Present Philosophical Tendencies* (1912) he examined the different provenances of theory and belief. One's belief, he thought, should change far more slowly than one's theory. Indeed, theories might change or be abandoned with very little cost or worry. Not so one's belief. To make this distinction more persuasive, Perry suggested that philosophers should use a special language – we would call it jargon – to prevent their theorizing from being mistaken for programmes of belief:

> I wish that philosophy, for theoretical purposes, might speak a language of its own, and settle its disputes in a vernacular that does not arrest the attention of the community. If this were possible, philosophy would be better entitled to the full benefit of that immunity from direct social responsibility which is most conducive to clear seeing and straight thinking. And society could afford to wait for the application of a more refined and better-tested truth.[14]

Perry's attitude in that passage is open to a cynical interpretation: that he wants philosophers to protect their mysteries and to keep them vested in the expert. I read it otherwise: that he wants philosophers to have the benefit of a free play of mind so that their theories will be judged upon considerations quite different from those which obtain in the market-place. Philosophers would not be inhibited, harassed, or tempted by a demand for the application of their vocabularies to political issues. Now Perry's distinction between theory and belief seems to me a valuable one, and it implies that while changes in one's belief should be made slowly and reluctantly, one's theories should be sought in a comparatively light or debonair style, speculative, experimental, and daring. What we are witnessing today is belief (or ideology) disguising itself as theory for immediate rhetorical advantage. I risk repeating myself by urging that we regard the work of theory as prolegomena toward the establishing of a concept – whatever the concept may be – and regard principles as finding their destiny in application of that concept and in the consequence of that application.

Let me now try to round out what I have been saying. Some of it is bound to be obvious, but there is no help for that. If I speak of principles, I mean those values in a writer's work which supposedly go without saying and are allowed to be judged upon their consequences. Bourgeois liberalism is for Rorty such a value. He does not regard it as needing exposition or defence; he takes it as self-evident, and puts it in the company of other words of high standing – citizenship, as a case in point. Other values are in need of justification, but not that one. So he uses bourgeois liberalism as the ground not of his beseeching but of his assertion. So much is clear. If Rorty's readers were of a sceptical bearing, they would regard as questionable any assertion, any stricture, that depended upon the prestige of the bourgeois liberalism he takes for granted.

It is harder to show what I mean by theory, or by the theorizing motive as distinct from the motive of principle and its application in particular cases. I shall mention one occasion and hope that it will make the small point.

On 28 April 1951 Wallace Stevens gave a talk at Mount

Holyoke College under the title 'Two or Three Ideas'. He
need not have been casual in the title: the ideas on show
numbered three:

> The first is that the style of a poem and the poem itself are
> one; the second is that the style of the gods and the gods
> themselves are one; the third is that in an age of disbelief,
> when the gods have come to an end, when we think of
> them as the aesthetic projections of a time that has passed,
> men turn to a fundamental glory of their own and from
> that create a style of bearing themselves in reality.[15]

These ideas in themselves do not amount to a theory.
Indeed, they are closer to being principles, in the sense
that they express the value – whether we call it humanism
or some other name – upon which Stevens's work is largely
based. They are principles, axioms, or prejudices. The best
that can be said for them is that they helped him to get
his work done. Stevens's readers are persuaded by them,
or they are not. But in either case they do not partake of
theory.

Where Stevens's lecture partakes of theory is in its
recourse to two words: 'style' and 'romantic'. Neither of
these is a commanding term. When we come upon the
word 'style' in Stevens's prose, as in his verse, we are
likely to deal with it glancingly and assume that it means
something more to him than it means to us. We take it as
pointing or gesturing toward a possible meaning, rather
than denoting a meaning comfortably in hand. That is to
say: the concept of style is not one of Stevens's principles,
if only because it is not sufficiently stable to count as a
value or a prejudice. It indicates the general area in which
Stevens is for the time being to be found, but not the
specific value he is enforcing. Much the same consideration
arises from 'romantic'. He first uses it near the beginning
of his talk, when he has quoted the first line of Baudelaire's
'La Vie antérieure' – '*J'ai longtemps habité sous de vastes*

portiques' – and supplied the first of two translations – 'A long time I lived beneath tremendous porches':

> The idea of an earlier life is, like the idea of a later life, or like the idea of a different life, part of the classic repertory of poetic ideas. It is part of one's inherited store of poetic subjects. Precisely, then, because it is traditional and because we understand its romantic nature and know what to expect from it, we are suddenly and profoundly touched when we hear it declaimed by a voice that says:
> I lived, for long, under huge porticoes.[16]

No voice says 'I lived, for long, under huge porticoes', especially if some voice has already said 'A long time I lived beneath tremendous porches'. Presumably Stevens wants us to think of the idea of an anterior life as if it occupied a space a little apart from Baudelaire's precise French words or anyone's imprecise English translation. When we hear Stevens saying 'and because we understand its romantic nature', we know that we don't understand what 'romantic' means in this context, spoken now for the first time. It is an x, worth whatever one deems it to be worth. Stevens doesn't define its value. He doesn't mention it again until his talk is almost over. But then it suffuses the entire paragraph. He has referred to a certain logic, and said that it must allow for a good many irrelevancies:

> One of the irrelevancies is the romantic. It looks like something completely contemptible in the light of literary intellectualism and cynicism. The romantic, however, has a way of renewing itself. It can be said of the romantic, just as it can be said of the imagination, that it can never effectively touch the same thing twice in the same way. It is partly because the romantic will not be what has been romantic in the past that it is preposterous to think of confining poetry hereafter to the revelation of reality. The whole effort of the imagination is toward the production of the romantic. When, therefore, the romantic is in abeyance,

when it is discredited, it remains true that there is always an unknown romantic and that the imagination will not be forever denied. There is something a little romantic about the idea that the style of a poem and the poem itself are one. It seems to be a much more broadly romantic thing to say that the style of the gods and the gods themselves are one. It is completely romantic to say that the style of men and men themselves are one. To collect and collate these ideas of disparate things may seem to pass beyond the romantic to the fantastic. I hope, however, that you will agree that if each one of these ideas is valid separately, or more or less valid, it is permissible to have brought them together as a collective source of suppositions. What is romantic in all of them is the idea of style which I have not defined in any sense uniformly common to all three. A poem is a restricted creation of the imagination.[17]

Much of the effect of that passage arises from our not knowing what Stevens means by 'romantic'; or rather, from our being willing to hold the word in a mobile – or even a notional – relation to his general theme. The theme is simple enough: it is what the poetic imagination can do in a time of unbelief. The word 'romantic' is not meaningless, but its meaning is not yet; it may take on a specific meaning as the sentences proceed, but Stevens doesn't promise as much. The mode of his use of the word is that of experiment. The closest he comes to a definition is that he distinguishes between 'the revelation of reality' and 'the production of the romantic'; between, shall we say, something that is already there in truth and something that may come into existence by a productive act of the imagination. The one is there, the other is not yet anywhere except as a possibility.

It is evident that a theory is being established, that it is a theory of the imagination, and that whatever Stevens means by 'romantic' is evidence in its favour – but only in favour of it as a possibility for the future. If 'the romantic' is not already in reality, it must be Stevens's name for a possibility in the mind that contemplates the world – contemplates it, however, with a view to the exercise of its own freedom in the world. It follows that 'the romantic' comes into being by *fiat* of the imagination, and in its form it appeases a particular desire of the imagination. 'The romantic' cannot be invoked or used as a principle, it does not yet exist. The little we know of it is that, when it comes into existence, it will exist somewhere between the revelation of reality and whatever extreme or bizarre imagery Stevens means by 'fantasy'. Unlike fantasy, it will accept some form of jurisdiction; it will not be merely wild.

Stevens's thinking in that passage is theoretic; it woos the crucial words 'romantic' and 'style', but it stops far short of requiring them to define themselves or otherwise to act as if they were already established as values or prejudices. This mode of thinking is experimental, unofficial, the discourse of an amateur in the play of mind and word. If the play were to become more arduous, it would aspire to a new theory of the poetic imagination, or an old theory made to appear new. It would be a theory largely in agreement with Kant and Coleridge, but with nuances achieved by taking other emphases into account: Valéry, Vaihinger, William James, Santayana. Meanwhile Stevens whispers among the choice words, letting them glance off one another. No script ordains these glances; they occur as they occur. So the style of theory is like that of improvisation: in the end, a form may appear, but meanwhile all we attend to is the taking of liberties.

NOTES

1 R. P. Blackmur, *Anni Mirabiles 1921–1925: Reason in the Madness of Letters* (Washington, D.C.: Library of Congress, 1956), p. 14.
2 Jacques Derrida, 'Some Statements and Truisms', in *The*

States of Theory: History, Art, and Critical Discourse (New York: Columbia University Press, 1990), p. 86.

3   Jacques Derrida, *The Truth in Painting*, tr. Geoffrey Bennington and Ian McLeod (Chicago: University of Chicago Press, 1987), pp. 107–8.

4   Leo Bersani, 'Against *Ulysses*', *Raritan* 8, no.2 (Fall 1988), pp. 20–1.

5   Emmanuel Levinas, *Totality and Infinity*, tr. Alphonso Lingis (Pittsburgh: Duquesne University Press, 1969), pp. 56–8.

6   Fredric Jameson, 'Wyndham Lewis as Futurist', *Hudson Review* 26, no. 2 (Summer 1973), p. 318.

7   Fredric Jameson, '*Ulysses* in History', in *James Joyce and Modern Literature*, eds W. J. McCormack and Alastair Steed (London: Routledge and Kegan Paul, 1982), pp. 128–9.

8   Paul de Man, *Blindness and Insight*, 2nd edn (Minneapolis: University of Minnesota Press, 1983), p. 262.

9   Ibid., p. 207.

10   Emmanuel Levinas, 'The Other Proust', in *The Levinas Reader*, ed. Sean Hand (Oxford: Blackwell, 1989), p. 165.

11   Richard Rorty, 'Foucault / Dewey / Nietzsche', *Raritan* 9, no. 4 (Spring 1990), p. 2.

12   *The Collected Poems of W. B. Yeats*, ed. Richard J. Finneran (New York: Macmillan Publishing Co., 1989), p. 348.

13   Alasdair MacIntyre, *After Virtue: A Study of Moral Theory* (London: Duckworth, 1981), p. 10.

14   Ralph Barton Perry, *Present Philosophical Tendencies* (New York: Longmans, Green, 1921), p. 22.

15   Wallace Stevens, *Opus Posthumous*, ed. Milton J. Bates (New York: Knopf, 1989), pp. 261–2.

16   Ibid., p. 258.

17   Ibid., p. 266.

Towards a Better Life

At the end of *The Voices of Silence*, André Malraux has come to terms with many works of art: paintings, sculptures, wall-drawings, artifacts from many diverse cultures. It is time for him to step back from these things and think of some force or quality they may have in common. In the final sentence he settles upon a formula which he probably doesn't regard as adequate; and yet it responds to the pressure of the entire book. The formula is 'Art is man's protest against his fate.' The formula is not self-evidently just. There are works of art – I am thinking of certain paintings by Paul Klee, but with further thought other works would occur to me – which seem to accept the human fate without protest; indeed, they celebrate the opportunities it provides. Still, I accept Malraux's formula as bearing upon many more works of art than can be accounted for by talk of celebration. 'Art is man's protest against his fate.' I shall be concerned more with the protest than the fate, and yet for that very reason I should acknowledge that many works of art and literature are concerned not so much with the fate as with our knowledge of it. There are many works which live in the service of that knowledge, even to the extent of letting the protest emerge as if in silence or between times. Art is one of the ways by which we come to know, or at least to divine, what our fate is, and it is a matter of emphasis whether the protest that issues from that knowledge is spoken or left implicit. When Ophelia in the third Act of the play sees Hamlet leave the stage, mad or with many signs of madness, and says

> O, woe is me
> T' have seen what I have seen, see what I see!

the point is moot whether she is crying out against the woe or living tense with the knowledge of it as itself ultimate and beyond redemption. There is grim consolation in knowing the worst and in living with that knowledge. In literature, we think of satire, burlesque, irony, elegy, the epic, and the naturalistic novel as genres with a particular gift for coming to know the human fate and for turning that knowledge into a kind of consolation. Tragedy is the form of our most complete knowledge of human fate, and it gathers human energy against it, not with any hope of circumventing it, but rather to set one force against another. The fact that the provoking force is categorical and impersonal doesn't make the responsive force absurd. Indeed, most tragedies make the conflict of these forces issue not only in the hero's death but in a sublime knowledge that precedes it. Similarly with the novel: much concerned with human fate and with the conditions that enforce it, the novel often exhibits an impulse to give that fate, in the end, a comelier name, and to construe it as in the long run somehow acceptable. Acceptable, perhaps, because it has brought forth a human response of extraordinary nobility.

For the moment, I am referring to the motive in literature which goes under various names and under any name tries to say what human life is like, what its conditions are, and what it seems to come to. We often call it representation, or *mimesis*, or even realism, and we think of these as denoting the attempt to name the categorical experience of being human and, by naming, to make sense of it. They mark a project of knowledge, and assume that, by coming to know our fate, we may the better put up with it, the knowledge being a sufficient incitement to stay the course. I take it that these expressive forms, being mimetic, are derived from the categories of resemblance and difference. There is indeed a risk of confounding their differences by speaking of them in the same breath. But they share certain axioms. They assume, to begin with, that there is nothing that does not originate in being. As Michel de Certeau has pointed out, realism is the genre which legitimizes discourse by its references. It is not at all neutral in that respect. On the contrary, it is injunctive, it signifies in the way in which a command is given; it demands to be believed, and claims to be merely taking dictation from the final authority in these matters, the way things are because of the way they have been and have become. A realistic novel is a construction of representations into laws imposed as if by the state of things. Novelists in this genre pretend that they are merely bearing witness to what has occurred. So it is rhetorically necessary that they conceal any indication of the conditions in which their representations are produced; they must somehow persuade the reader, at least for the duration of the novel, that these events really happened, as if spontaneously or by the imperative of nature. We are reading against the spirit of these novels if we keep reminding ourselves that they are discourses like any other, or that their claims to self-evident truth are self-evidently false. We are breaking the contract. Sometimes a novelist breaks it, and it is a cause of scandal to readers who care for the conventions and the proprieties. Henry James was shocked to find Trollope taking 'a suicidal satisfaction in reminding the reader that the story he was telling was only, after all, a make-believe'.[1]

But I should not give the impression that the realistic novel has a monopoly on being and knowledge, or on art as man's protest against his fate. In 'Among School Children' Yeats presents it as fateful that the images we project from our desire can never be satisfactory objects of that desire, if only because it is endless and exorbitant. The images projected by mothers, lovers, and nuns are merely what they are; they can't change merely to meet and appease the desire that constituted them. Besides, the mind that projected the images is already changing into another form or phase of itself. It has been argued that Yeats found in Gentile's *The Reform of Education* (1922) a discursive passage about human fate, and that it impelled him to meditate upon the value of images and the limited character of that value. Gentile writes:

> The spirit's being is its alteration. The more it *is*, – that is, the more it becomes, the more it lives, – the more difficult it is for it to recognise itself in the object. It might therefore be said that he who increases his knowledge also increases his ignorance, if he is unable to trace this knowledge back to its origin, and if the spirit's rally does not induce him to rediscover himself at the bottom of the object, which has been allowed to alter and alienate itself more and more from the secret source of its own becoming. Thus it happens, as was said of old, that 'He that increaseth knowledge increaseth sorrow.' All human sorrow proceeds from our incapacity to recognise ourselves in the object, and consquently to feel our own infinite liberty.[2]

There are many Yeatsian themes in that passage, but the most telling one, in its bearing upon 'Among School Children',[3] is that man's fate includes the categorical discrepancy between desire and its images. We project our desires into images, but cannot find our freedom in them; while we are creating them, we are changing, our desires are changing. The child is changing while his mother is changing, but in different and incompatible ways. In the last two stanzas of Yeats's poem the discrepancy is so emphatic that the images of desire become 'self-born mockers of man's enterprise', even though they have symbolized 'all heavenly glory':

> Both nuns and mothers worship images,
> But those the candles light are not as those
> That animate a mother's reveries,
> But keep a marble or a bronze repose.
> And yet they too break hearts – O Presences
> That passion, piety or affection knows,
> And that all heavenly glory symbolise –
> O self-born mockers of man's enterprise.

The sense doesn't coincide with the end of that stanza; the invocation is incomplete. The capitalized Presences must be the images of desire as projected by mothers, lovers, and nuns – they correspond to the affection, passion, and piety by which they are known. They are Presences because the images of desire have taken up their ghostly station. If they mock man's enterprise, it can only be because they know how inadequate they are to the desires that promulgated them. They know that they would be adequate only if the desiring mind found itself fully in them and enjoyed its freedom in that recognition.

In the last stanza, Yeats specifies the conditions that would have to be satisfied before the human subject could enjoy that freedom:

> Labour is blossoming or dancing where
> The body is not bruised to pleasure soul,
> Nor beauty born out of its own despair,
> Nor blear-eyed wisdom out of midnight oil.

Here Yeats is looking back to his early poem 'Adam's Curse' and to his first acknowledgement of time and body as instruments of that curse. In the last lines of 'Among School Children' it is a matter of dispute whether he finds the curse removable, on the evidence of dances, dancers, and chestnut trees, or imposed again by the impossibility of distinguishing between dancer and dance:

> O chestnut tree, great rooted blossomer,
> Are you the leaf, the blossom or the bole?

> O body swayed to music, O brightening glance,
> How can we know the dancer from the dance?

I can't produce a good reason, least of all a good Yeatsian reason, for even thinking of reducing the organic unity of a chestnut tree to leaf, blossom, or bole, or for making a puzzled choice between these, or for wanting to distinguish between dancer and dance, or to infer the dancer from the dance. John Hollander has argued, in *Melodious Guile*, that in these several rhetorical questions, Yeats is producing figures 'of conceptual inadequacy in dealing with Process'.[4] I find this suggestion helpful, and I deduce from it – and from Gentile's paragraph – that the subject is always encountered in its changing, and the object, too, in its changing, and that there is discrepancy on every side of the question. At all events, 'Among School Children' takes its place beside several poems which protest not against this or that historical consideration but against man's fate as such.

I have looked at 'Among School Children' as a poem that tries to know what man's fate is, and to derive some consolation from the knowledge. It is a poem that depends not only upon what Yeats knows, but upon the degree to which he holds that knowledge in common with his readers. He does not argue us into agreement with him; he relies upon us to compare his sense of the world with our own. He is counting upon us to know what life is like, the conditions it imposes, the discrepancy it inevitably entails. Even if he believes, as he writes in 'The Statues', that 'knowledge increases unreality, that / Mirror on mirror mirrored is all the show', he accepts the privilege of knowledge in the present poem. We accept it, too. It would undermine the force of the poem if at any point we felt impelled to say of its argument: 'No, it isn't true.' Levinas has pointed out that in our tradition, veritable thought is true thought, and that knowing is thinking referred to being. This explains why the appeal of representation, of *mimesis*, is so strong. It is impossible to get away from representation for very long, if only because our definitions of knowledge and of meaning are alike referred to being, and because our languages have an incorrigible interest in that reference.

It is evident that language has a representational capacity, and indeed that it cultivates a prejudice in favour of representation. So far as I am aware, this is agreed; no critic, least of all Jacques Derrida, has disputed it. The disputes arise after the agreement, when more extreme claims are made. In our tradition the relation between thought and being has been so binding that it has been nearly impossible to separate them. So difficult, in fact, that – as Levinas has noted – when Kant separated them and discovered meanings not subject to reality, he regarded those meanings as defective, empty of the things they aimed at. He continued to measure them against the being they lacked or disavowed. I will come back to Kant in a moment, because my concern is not with representation – that can enforce itself – but with certain possibilities on the far side of it or beyond it. These are possibilities of fiction, or rather of fictiveness.

There is indeed a tradition according to which the fictive capacity of the mind is valued, but valued as providing relaxation after a hard day that has been governed by stricter determinations. In the second book of the *De Augmentis*, for instance, Bacon ascribes the fictive capacity to poetry and says that it 'raises the mind aloft, accommodating the shows of things to the desires of the mind, not (like reason and history) buckling and bowing down the mind to the nature of things'.[5] Bacon doesn't dispute that the nature of things is what it is, and that it is vouched for by reason and history. But he claims that there is another capacity of mind – we would call it 'imagination', and think it expressed itself in fictions – designed to mitigate the severity of nature as reported by reason and history. Sidney's *Defence of Poesy* proposes much the same accommodation. Reason and history are allowed to have privileged access to nature and being, and to veridical knowledge as Levinas describes it, turned upon being. It would be a conceit to claim equal status for the reports of reason and of imagination; they have the status of work and of play; of reality and of an intermittent and temporary escape from its imperatives. So it is hardly surprising that when Kant recognizes the possibility of an aesthetic idea and sets it free from the control of concepts, he is wary of this freedom and thinks it may amount to a disability. 'By an aesthetic idea', he says in the *Critique of Aesthetic Judgement*, 'I mean that representation of the imagination which induces much thought, yet without the possibility of any definite thought whatever, i.e. *concept*, being adequate to it.'[6] The imagination, to Kant, is the mind's power of invention, or producing what nature has not given, a distinctive *copia* free and freely enjoyed, independent of concepts. It follows that art is exempt from determinant or cognitive judgement, the judgement by virtue of which thinking is turned upon being. Art is not grounded on concepts, or intentionally directed toward them. The definition of knowledge as thinking turned upon being must have remarkable power if Kant thinks fictiveness a dubious or otherwise defective capacity.

Schiller got over any misgiving he might have felt on that score by appealing to the notion of play as an act of the mind superior to both the impulse to sense and the impulse to form, remedying the deficiencies of each. Man is only and completely man when he is at play. And the source of play is superfluity, the excess of energy which permits people to extend their enjoyment 'beyond every need'. Indeed, the most persuasive theory of aesthetics is based upon the understanding that it is this excess, this *copia* of energy, which takes the form of art. Not art as sublimation of blocked energies but as – it is Lyotard's phrasing – 'concentrations of libidinal energy on the surfaces of the visible and the articulable'.[7] It is not clear to me why these energies must be libidinal. It seems more reasonable to suppose, with Goethe in his letter to Louise Seidler (February 1818) on the relief of *Phigalia*, that these energies may be recognized as the emotions of hope, anticipation, and astonishment. The condition of art, according to Goethe, is probability, 'but within the realm of probability the highest ideal must be supplied which does not otherwise appear'.[8]

Having referred to Schiller and to Lyotard, it doesn't seem premature to invoke the notion implied by the title of my lecture: towards a better life. The title refers to an early work of fiction by Kenneth Burke, in which 'towards a better life' is deemed to mean 'towards comedy'. But I propose to extend the gesture somewhat by claiming that the first step towards a better life, in art, is by releasing art from the duty of representation. I have conceded that the release can't be complete; that the duty is too intimately recognized in the structure of our languages to be given up.   But we are under no obligation to think that the work of art is merely dutiful, or that its only destiny is to refer to something other than itself. It is entirely possible to claim, with Lyotard, that the mode of existence of a work of art is not vicarious; it is not there because something else is absent or missing. It is there because a certain concentration of energy, in excess of appetitive need, is available at a particular point. It is just as reasonable to think of this concentration of energy as turned toward a possible future as it is to assume that it must be turned toward an actual or hypothetical past. The work of art, in that light, gives hope a form and declares it possible. A poem or a novel is an object added to the world; it is not there in place of anything lost or missing.

It is my prejudice that there is a certain propriety in thinking in these terms at the moment. Many readers seem to feel that a certain phase in the history of philosophy and perhaps in the history of literature has reached a point of misgiving, if not of embarrassment. I do not mean that we have passed from modernity to post-modernity; indeed, these words seem to me nearly useless, mere tokens of our desire to feel that we are involved in a dramatic moment. I see no evidence that we are. The only dramatic consideration I am aware of is the sense that official forms of thinking are not self-evidently useful ones. It is clear that a few philosophers are doubting the wisdom of continuing their activities along the same lines. I note in Levinas's *Otherwise than Being* and Habermas's *The Philosophical Discourse of Modernity* that the philosophy of consciousness is under severe interrogation. Nobody is questioning the merit of an era in the history of philosophy which includes Kant, Hegel, Schiller, Nietzsche, Husserl, Heidegger, Derrida, and Foucault. But the assumption that philosophy must continue to be preoccupied with knowledge, and with the definition of knowledge as thinking turned upon being, is indeed open – being opened – to question. Levinas is even more demanding in this matter than Habermas. He construes modernity as 'the consciousness of a certain definitively acquired freedom'. It would appear that there is no break between the project of modernity and the project of the Enlightenment: they have a shared purpose in keeping to the aim of knowledge, that of 'comprehending the world and the past in terms of *being* which knowledge assimilates'. Modernity is the latest phase of the Enlightenment, the moment in which the freedom of knowledge is unlimited. Levinas has noted that modernity and its freedom, whether through critical analyses of social facts or through psychoanalytical studies 'are always in correlation with the institutional existence of science, methods, and manipulations of the given'.[9] The aim, in every case, is the appropriation of personal and social life, on the analogy of the appropriation of natural forces by science and technology.

I do not claim to know whether these appropriations have been completed or not. But I have been impressed by Levinas's argument that in retaining a metaphysics of the will we should not retain it as a will-to-knowledge or, the same thing, a will-to-power. The fundamental act, to him, is that by which one person recognizes and welcomes another; the jurisdiction entailed is that of justice, the principles engaged are those of ethics. Rules of logic are never called upon to sustain the primordial act of acknowledging another person. Levinas's formula for this is: ethics precedes ontology. I don't think he means that ethics precedes ontology merely as a logical or categorical necessity, but as a primordial act by virtue of which we acknowledge the humanity we share with others. For that reason, Levinas opposes the device by which ethical acts would be subjected to the strictures of reason and logic, as if those forces needed only to be patient, knowing that they would win in the end. 'There is no point', Levinas argues in *Totality and Infinity*, 'in formally distinguishing will from understanding; will from reason; when you decide at once to consider as good will only the will that adheres to clear ideas, or that makes decisions only out of respect for the universal.' If acts of the ethical will are accompanied by anything in Levinas's account of them, it is by 'the primordial face-to-face of language'.[10]

If we bring together these two considerations – the release of language, however partial that release, from the duty of representing and the primacy of ethics – we give language the right not to be tied to knowledge and being. It is not our business to tell writers what they should do with this freedom; or even to instruct readers that they should regard words as 'symbolic actions' – it is Kenneth Burke's phrase – rather than as vehicles of knowledge. But readers might usefully reconsider the privilege traditionally given to metaphor and metonymy, which are figures of likeness and difference, and therefore still tied to being and knowledge. I note that some critics have indeed been turning their interest away from metaphor and metonymy and reflecting upon prosopopoeia, the figure by which one summons an absent – or indeed non-existent – figure to appear. You may say that this figure is still tied to being and knowledge, but I am not sure that it is; one can summon a flute-playing centaur or some rough beast of no recognizable species slouching toward Bethlehem to be born. I would not try to insist on this, but I support the drift of criticism away from metaphor and metonymy. I support, too, much of the theory of speech acts, except that I would hope to find it acknowledging the priority of language in its collective sense. In Saussure's terms, *langue* precedes *parole*, and provides the conditions within which a speech act is possible.

What these considerations suggest is, on the reader's part, a philosophy of symbolic action and a corresponding aesthetics. It is difficult, these days, to use the word 'aesthetic' at all; it regularly incurs a charge of frivolity, or indeed of bad faith. Think of the animosity with which fascism is regularly described as the application of aesthetic criteria to politics; regardless of the fact that aesthetics means perception, and that an aesthetic experience is just that, an experience of perception. A work of art is an object created for perception, and sequestered in that consideration from every other use to which it may be put. Susanne Langer is right when she speaks of all artistic elements as 'virtual, created only for perception'.[11] It is difficult to say even as much as that without incurring a further charge of wanting to remove works of art from every social, economic, and political consideration. In a sense, that is precisely what I want to do, if only to be able to say that a work of art is not an editorial or a letter to the Editor; it is a form, the trace of a symbolic act, and as a form it exists only to be perceived. An aesthetic theory is a set of considerations which enable us to understand what such a form is, and what is entailed by its presenting itself to us for perception alone.

It would be reasonable to maintain, according to a tradition of aesthetic judgement from Kant to Langer, that the pleasure of the aesthetic experience is intrinsic, and that it is made available by removing the work of art from the ordinary possessive or opportunistic forms of attention we bring to our consideration of objects. We could then say that the aesthetic experience is valuable because it brings into play those capacities in us which are otherwise set aside by more aggressive motives. But it would be a difficult matter to determine whether or not this satisfaction is an exception to the otherwise universal rule which I mentioned in relation to Gentile and Yeats: the rule according to which all human sorrow arises from our incapacity to recognize ourselves in the object, as for instance the Yeatsian images of desire. There is indeed a certain margin of disagreement in this matter. Gentile maintains that we can't recognize ourselves in the objects we attend to, and therefore can't enjoy our liberty in their vicinity. But Valéry argues that this arises not from man's incapacity but from his refusal. The self, according to Valéry in the 'Analecta, Tel Quel II', 'flees all created things, it withdraws from negation to negation: one might give the name "Universe" to everything in which the self refuses to recognize itself'.[12] The difference between Valéry and Gentile is that Valéry grants – or appears to – that the self would willingly recognize itself in those objects or images which it has made, propelled by its desire; Gentile, as I read him, would insist that even then there is no possibility of recognition or of freedom.

But there is one version of the aesthetic experience which is more concessive than either Gentile's or Valéry's. In *The Aesthetic Dimension* Marcuse argues that Marxist orthodoxy has gone wrong in interpreting the quality and truth of a work of art in terms of the prevailing relations of production. He maintains, on the contrary, that art, by virtue of its aesthetic form, is largely autonomous *vis-à-vis* the given social relations. Literature is revolutionary, he argues, 'only with reference to itself, as content having become form'. Indeed, he goes further, and asserts that Marxism has erred in putting a low value upon subjectivity, not only upon the rational subject but upon inwardness, emotions, and imagination. It was a mistake to dissolve the subjectivity of individuals into class consciousness; because the need for radical change 'must be rooted in the subjectivity of individuals themselves, in their intelligence and passions, their drives and their goals'. Marxists should have seen that the world formed by art is not at all inauthentic, but the very reality that is distorted and suppressed in the given reality. It follows that 'the critical function of art . . . resides in the aesthetic form'. This does not produce a false consciousness, but rather a counter-consciousness: 'a negation of the realist-conformist mind'. The truth of art consists 'in its power to break the monopoly of established power – that is, of those who established it – to *define* what is *real*'. Only if art is withdrawn from 'the mystifying power of the given' can it free itself to express its own truth. The supreme merit of art is that it contradicts the version of reality that obtains in social and economic life.[13]

The whole purpose of Marcuse's book is to defend the freedom of art by assigning high value to the freedom it imagines. Like Ernst Bloch, Marcuse turns that freedom toward a future, utopian if we want to call it that, but not a whit the worse for such a designation. So it is not at all misleading to bring together Kant, Schiller, Marcuse, Levinas, and de Certeau in this consideration: that if the poem is not legitimized by the order of its reference, it legitimizes a different space and reveals its possibility 'in the very excess of what imposes itself'. This gesture, de Certeau maintains, 'belongs equally to aesthetics and to ethics': the difference between them is slight, 'as the aesthetic is essentially the appearance or the form of ethics in the domain of language'.[14] The gesture rejects the authority of the fact, transgresses the social convention which demands that 'the real' be law. It follows that the discourse of art is not under any obligation to have knowledge or to turn knowledge upon what merely exists. Ethics defines a space between what is and what ought to be. So does aesthetics.

Marcuse wants us to regard the images of art as indeed tokens of desire, but specifically our desire for freedom, and most of all the freedom to imagine a better life. I am content with that. But to guard against the risk that the utopia of art may be written off as mere day-dreaming or fantasy, it would be prudent to say that the images of art need not be tokens of the artist's desire. They may issue from the artist's sense of the internal possibilities of the medium. It is entirely possible that in a Joycean epiphany the real may be disclosed in the midst of mundane being. It is also possible that an internal epiphany may be come upon, in which the artist realizes a creative possibility of form and texture. The warm reality and the offered good may be found in the world, even in 'a flat world of changing lights and noise'; and the writer's response to these felicities may well take the form of representation or celebration. But such joys may be found within the medium, the language. In Eliot's 'Animula', for instance, – the lines

Leaving disordered papers in a dusty room;
Living first in the silence of the viaticum.

– the precise emphasis upon 'living', what it means in its spiritual relation to 'first' and 'silence' and 'viaticum', is intimated by its emergence from 'leaving', from the choice of leaving not only the disordered papers but the assured, certain certainties of a facile belief, an ostensibly positive achievement enjoyed before the soul should be ready to enjoy it; it is a vulgarity. It is a coincidence that the English language places 'living' in the phonetic vicinity of 'leaving'; but Eliot, observing the coincidence, makes a poetic much of it. It doesn't matter to us whether we think he stumbled upon it or steadied himself in finding it. He had, however, a notion to sustain him, his trust – short of confidence –

in the 'primitive power of the Word' – a sense of capacities, mainly reverberant and therefore implicative, which words have, even before they make the specific commitments embodied in grammar and syntax. He thought of it in association with Poe, Tennyson, Mallarmé, and Swinburne; but also in relation to Shakespeare and the Jacobean tragic dramatists.

But I should now produce two or three samples; they are nothing more than that: not sublimities, but occasions on which writers discover possibilities within the medium of the English language which release them, for the time being, from the office of representation into the mercy of fictiveness.

Samuel Beckett is propelling Watt in an easterly direction, on foot; it is a matter of legs and knees:

> So, standing first on one leg, and then on the other, he moved forward, a headlong tardigrade, in a straight line. The knees, on these occasions, did not bend. They could have, but they did not. No knees could better bend than Watt's, when they chose, there was nothing the matter with Watt's knees, as may appear. But when out walking they did not bend, for some obscure reason. Notwithstanding this, the feet fell, heel and sole together, flat upon the ground, and left it, for the air's uncharted ways, with manifest repugnancy. The arms were content to dangle, in perfect equipendency.[15]

On the rare occasions of its use, the word 'tardigrade' means someone who moves slowly; in zoology it refers to a member of the family of edentate – that is, toothless – mammals comprising the sloths. So Watt is a sloth. His being 'a headlong tardigrade' means that he spends most of his time of motion in a headlong posture, this condition amounting to little in the way of movement. It is a mark of Beckett's common style that it reduces the organism called Watt to an articulated system of knees and feet, and then goes some distance to make up for the reduction by assigning residual and largely independent motivation to these organs. The knees did not choose to bend. Indeed, the mechanical movements of knees and feet are directed upon their rudimentary way until Beckett discovers within the articulations of his sentence a possibility he is impelled to welcome; it is embodied in the phrase 'for the air's uncharted ways'. Nothing in the narrative office of the sentence requires it. Let me recite it again:

> Notwithstanding this, the feet fell, heel and sole together, flat upon the ground, and left it, for the air's uncharted ways, with manifest repugnancy.

No duty of representation is fulfilled in the interpolated phrase; for proof, omit the phrase and you won't notice any defect in the representation. It is the sentence, not Watt, that seeks the air's uncharted ways – as well it might.

Another sample, another indication of a moment in which a writer seizes upon a fictive possibility come upon in the otherwise officious course of the work in hand, is found in Philip Larkin's poem 'High Windows', in which we are to imagine perhaps a late-middle-aged man looking at a couple of young lovers and envying their sexual freedom; then he thinks about himself, a generation or more back:

> I wonder if
> Anyone looked at me, forty years back,
> And thought, *That'll be the life;*
> *No God any more, or sweating in the dark*
>
> *About hell and that, or having to hide*
> *What you think of the priest. He*
> *And his lot will all go down the long slide*
> *Like free bloody birds*. And immediately
>
> Rather than words comes the thought of high windows:
> The sun-comprehending glass,
> And beyond it, the deep blue air, that shows
> Nothing, and is nowhere, and is endless.[16]

If the laws of representation were in force, that phrase 'the sun-comprehending glass' could not pass. The glass of windows, however high, does not comprehend the sun; even if the glass were the modern kind, found in certain sun-glasses and in many high-rise buildings, which seems to dominate the light by refusing to let it through. The phrase that may help us is 'Rather than words', which I take to mean 'Rather than more words of the same kind as I've been speaking and quoting, discursive, envious words'. So the thought of high windows is called upon not only to bring the poem to an end but to put a stop to the discourse of invidious comparison between one generation and another. Instead of discourse, then, we have an image, a pure presentation, as far removed as possible from argument. The phrase 'the sun-comprehending glass' is justified not because the glass comprehends the sun but because it seems to the speaker to do so: all the better if the task of comprehending the sun is handed over to glass that seems unintimidated by it. The release of consigning the task to the windows is extended beyond them to the sky that doesn't have to reflect anything.

I should repeat that I do not see any conflict in literature between the duty of representing the world and the gratification of choosing as far as possible not to represent it. Our words are referential whether we like it or not. But it is a matter of choice whether a writer will endorse the referential character of the words or play fast and loose with it. I confess a prejudice in favour of fictions which offer to tell us not what life is like but what a better life would be like. If we want a little formula to stand for this motive, I offer a phrase from Dryden, where he writes of 'moving the sleeping images of things toward the light'. I have a second prejudice to go along with the first; that these sleeping images are to be found in the echoes and recesses of a language, and that they may have the force of a revelation among the words.

In Larkin's poem, 'words' issues by right of rhyme

from 'birds'. The simile 'like free bloody birds' is bold, because children going down a long slide aren't free; even while the going is good, the pleasure is one of not being free, for the few seconds the slide takes. The freedom is taken in the words of the simile itself, the vulgar emphasis of 'bloody', which has nothing to do with the birds but with one's freedom-taking in language. One is free to be unpointedly vulgar among the words. The freedom then extends itself from the birds to the high windows which, often, only birds can see, and the pleasure expressed in the rest of the poem is that of a vacation exercise; it is the pleasure of releasing thoughts from words, glass from having to be seen through, air from having to contain anything or to end anywhere. In 'High Windows' Larkin is inviting readers to imagine the pleasure of seeing words not filled with meaning but emptied of the responsibility of meaning; going on vacation, to feel the exhilaration in 'Nothing', 'nowhere', and 'endless'.

Among the many weak points of my argument, one especially embarrasses me. Suppose someone were to say: 'I grant you the possibility of evading, at least to some extent, the duty of representing the way things are, all the things (as James conceded) we can't help meeting and knowing. It follows that the fictive intention shows a different life from our daily one. But why should I suppose that in addition to being different it is also better? It is not necessarily better to the extent of its being different.'

Let me take, as a case in emphasized point, *What Maisie Knew*, a novel that has lately come in for much discussion in an ethical context. In *Versions of Pygmalion* (1990) J. Hillis Miller has acted upon a promise he made in *The Ethics of Reading* (1987), to examine 'the law of the ethics of reading' in several provocative instances. *What Maisie Knew* is one of these, appropriately, since what Maisie knows is the ground of what she does: her decision in the end not to stay with Sir Claude and Mrs Beale but to return to London with her governess, Mrs Wix. I will remind you of the story in its merest outline. Beale Farange and his wife Ida have an only child, Maisie. We don't know what age Maisie is; there is a reference to her being six, or rather to her having been six, but we are not told how many years the domestic and adulterous entanglements of Beale and Ida traverse. By the time Maisie comes to make her decision, she might be nearly any small age, given the precocity of James's fictive children; she might be perhaps nine or ten or eleven. In any event, she has come to know a lot about her parents: that they hate each other; that they have formed, each of them, several other sexual relationships which entail absences, rejections, claims, counter-claims, repudiations. One of Beale's lovers is Miss Overmore, and during the course of the novel they marry and are predictably unhappy, unfaithful, and devious. Ida, too, has married one of her lovers, Sir Claude, and been unfaithful to him with a long list of men. Sir Claude and Miss Overmore – now Mrs Beale – become sexually involved, and if further divorces could be achieved, they would, at least at certain moments, wish to marry. Meanwhile they want Maisie to live with them. Such an arrangement, scandalous indeed, is violently opposed by Mrs Wix, still a mere governess, but a most formidable one.

James's plan, as he explained it in the Preface to the novel, was to make virtue flourish in conditions notably squalid; to preserve Maisie from the sordidness of her environment:

> the small expanding consciousness would have to be saved, have to become presentable as a register of impressions; and saved by the experience of certain advantages, by some enjoyed profit and some achieved confidence, rather than coarsened, blurred, sterilised, by ignorance and pain.[17]

Why would James wish to fly in the face of the probability that Maisie would turn out to be tainted by her parents and their adulterous company? 'For satisfaction of the mind': that is the shortest version of James's reason, and it is nearly sufficient; it points, like the reasons given by Bacon and by Sidney, to the animating motive of fiction, to hold out the possibility of a better life. That Maisie should be nearly as corrupt as her parents is a probability in the nature, or rather the culture, of the case. That she should turn out to be the torch of virtue is not probable, but possible; and James imagines this possibility and tries to make it appear a feasible happiness. Maisie is as James shows her to be, because to show her otherwise, as sharing to the full the social world of her parents and accepting its commerce, would be morally intolerable to him.

We can describe this situation in various ways. Nearly the simplest is to call it an instance of irony, according to James's description of that imaginative act in the Preface to *The Lesson of the Master*. Asked where on earth he found his supersubtle fry, his Neil Paradays, Ralph Limberts, Hugh Verekers, and so forth, James answered, in effect, that he imagined them in default of their existing. The strength of applied irony, he maintained, is in the sincerities, the lucidities, the utilities that stand behind it:

> When it's not a campaign, of a sort, on behalf of the something better (better than the obnoxious, the provoking object) that blessedly, as is assumed, *might* be, it's not worth speaking of. But this is exactly what we mean by operative irony. It implies and projects the possible other case, the case rich and edifying where the actuality is pretentious and vain . . . to imagine, in a word, the honourable, the producible case.[18]

James uses the opportunity of his fiction to 'create the record' in default of any evidence of 'the something better' he could produce merely by looking around him.

What corresponds, in Maisie, to operative irony in James

is 'wonder': he gives it this name throughout the novel and again in the Preface. About Maisie's sense of the shallow people who surround her, James says that 'she has simply to wonder. . . . about them, and they begin to have meanings, aspects, solidities, connexions – connexions with the "universal" – that they could scarce have hoped for'. Beale, Ida, and their associates would not be worth looking at were it not for Maisie's wondering about them and the consequence for us of that wondering. James speaks of 'the rich little spectacle of objects embalmed in her wonder'.

But these refrences don't quite explain themselves. To be embalmed, one has to be in some sense dead, and then to be in some sense preserved. Operative irony is sustained by one's knowing more than the evidence on show; knowing, for instance, that what is on show doesn't exhaust the possibilities of the case. In Maisie, wonder seems to entail not knowing the evidence, not knowing all of it or what the facts on show mean, and yet somehow divining a something better than what appears. The *OED* isn't much help with wonder, except that it suggests that there is a note of *A Midsummer Night's Dream* in its vicinity. An element in wonder is the willingness not to draw conclusions from the evidence, or not to draw them immediately. There will be time. In Maisie it goes along with the habit which James makes much of, her policy of appearing to be stupid rather than answer directly to each proffered occasion. She conceals whatever she knows, and makes of herself a second self to be produced, perhaps, later. The fact that I speak of it as a policy shows that it's a questionable device. It could easily tell against Maisie by making her seem just as devious as the wretches she has to deal with. But it's easy to give her whatever allowance she needs, her conditions being so appalling, her need to protect herself so acute.

Miller's questions about *What Maisie Knew* suggest themselves at this point. The main issue turns upon the quality of Maisie's moral sense. The whole drama of the

novel, indeed, turns on Maisie's capacity to hold the torch
of virtue, pulled back and forth as she is by the adults in
her vicinity and by her feelings, dangerously intense, for
some of them. In Chapter 26, Mrs Wix comes to doubt
that Maisie has a moral sense at all; it appears to have been
killed off by Sir Claude and Maisie's love of him. The
terrible doubt arose for Mrs Wix, I think, when Maisie
asked: 'Why after all should we have to choose between
you? Why shouldn't we be four?'[19] That is: Why shouldn't
Mrs Beale and Sir Claude live together and have Mrs Wix
and Maisie with them? The fact that Maisie asks such a
question makes for Mrs Wix every evidence of a catastrophe: it means that Maisie hasn't a moral sense, can't see
the horror of this arrangement. Till late in the novel, Maisie
hasn't had to think of having a moral sense or even of
knowing what it might be. Mrs Wix's questions at least
make Maisie know that the phrase evidently means something; though what, she could not say. Mrs Wix knows
what it is; it is a treasure that may be lost, or a seed that
may be 'nipped in the bud'. This latter is what she accuses
Sir Claude of having done to Maisie's moral sense. The
crucial passage is the one Miller chooses for explication.
Mrs Wix is interrogating Maisie, with Mrs Beale and Sir
Claude standing by:

'Your moral sense. *Haven't* I, after all, brought it out?' She
spoke as she had never spoken even in the schoolroom and
with the book in her hand.
   It brought back to the child's recollection how she sometimes couldn't repeat on Friday the sentence that had been
glib on Wednesday, and she dealt all feebly and ruefully
with the present tough passage. Sir Claude and Mrs Beale
stood there like visitors at an 'exam'. She had indeed in an
instant a whiff of the faint flower that Mrs Wix pretended
to have plucked and now with such a peremptory hand
thrust at her nose. Then it left her, and, as if she were
sinking with a slip from a foothold, her arms made a short
jerk. What this jerk represented was the spasm within her

of something still deeper than a moral sense. She looked
at her examiner; she looked at the visitors; she felt the
rising of the tears she had kept down at the station. They
had nothing – no, distinctly nothing – to do with her moral
sense. The only thing was the old flat shameful schoolroom
pleas. 'I don't know – I don't know.'

'Then you've lost it.' Mrs Wix seemed to close the book
as she fixed the straighteners on Sir Claude. 'You've nipped
it in the bud. You've killed it when it had begun to live.'[20]

Miller's commentary on this passage concentrates on its
three main metaphors: the child being examined on her
lessons in school, the flower thrust under one's nose as
something to be smelled, the slip or fall as from a cliff or
hill. The commentary is, as one has come to expect, responsive and responsible. But it leaves, I think, a little more to
be said about the 'spasm within her of something still
deeper than a moral sense'. Miller interprets the spasm as
a convulsion of feeling, mainly erotic, aroused by Maisie's
fear of losing Sir Claude, whom she wants for herself. Our
not knowing what age Maisie is allows us to feel that she
is old enough to have erotic feelings and to have them
aroused by her stepmother's lover. A spasm is indeed a
muscular convulsion or throe. That it is a sign of erotic
violence, it is impossible either to claim or to deny. The
only evidence we have is provided by the narrator. Now
the narrator is not a character, a presence, in the novel,
but he or she often intervenes, often says 'I', commenting.
In the Preface, James defends this procedure by saying
that Maisie, like other children, has much experience, but
not the words, the terms, by which it would be understood
and conveyed; so the narrator is justified in finding the
words for her and taking advantage of her relations and
activities 'better than she herself'. The narrator doesn't tell
us what the 'something still deeper than a moral sense' is.
The next sentence, about Maisie's rising tears, is only a
little way beyond what she might have conveyed of the

occasion. But the sentence then following marks the narrator's intervention again, saying of the tears, 'They had nothing – no, distinctly nothing – to do with her moral sense.' How are we to take this? It is so emphatic in its repeated 'nothing' that one would think someone had proposed a rival interpretation: that Maisie's tears were indeed caused by her moral sense, belated as its arrival is and now the cause of regret, muddlement, bewilderment. Still, we must obey this narrator; not always adequate to the occasion, he or she is at least reliable.

Is it necessary to say, if only because Miller doesn't say it, that there are several 'somethings' deeper than a moral sense? A moral sense may or may not be innate – it is arguable, and continues to be argued – but it is probably wise to think of it as a cultural acquisition, as it clearly enough is in Maisie. It would make light of the novel if we were to take the moral of the story to be: it doesn't matter what scoundrels your parents are, provided you have Mrs Wix for governess. It is a modern prejudice that virtually everything is a cultural acquisition, that nothing comes directly or, as we say, in an unmediated form from nature. If the something is still deeper than a moral sense, it must be very deep; as deep as the body's determination to survive, or its dread of dissolution. James didn't share the modern prejudice I have mentioned, any more than he shared the prejudice according to which we have no feelings, sentiments, desires separable from the words that establish them for us. He believed that Maisie has experiences for which she lacks the words. The spasm is a sign of any feeling for which she lacks the words. The words she would need, on this occasion, would enable her to discriminate between several rival considerations, forces of attraction nearly equal. So she can only weep and cry, 'I don't know, I don't know.'

But we are not done yet. We haven't even come to Miller's questions. There is another piece of evidence.

When Mrs Wix accuses Sir Claude of having nipped Maisie's moral sense in the bud, we have his answer in this passage:

> She was a newer Mrs Wix than ever, a Mrs Wix high and great; but Sir Claude was not after all to be treated as a little boy with a missed lesson. 'I've not killed anything,' he said; 'on the contrary I think I've produced life. I don't know what to call it – I haven't even known how decently to deal with it, to approach it; but, whatever it is, it's the most beautiful thing I've ever met – it's exquisite, it's sacred.'[21]

Sir Claude is referring to the bargain Maisie had offered him, that she would give up Mrs Wix if he would give up Mrs Beale. He had refused, but he regarded Maisie's offer of the bargain as exquisite; like some lovely work of art or of nature that had suddenly been set down among them, as the narrator comments. A page or two later the narrator reports:

> He was rapidly recovering himself on this basis of fine appreciation. 'She made her condition – with such a sense of what it should be! She made the only right one.'[22]

The word 'life' in the speech of Sir Claude which I have quoted is required to take a great strain. The claim he makes is extraordinary, that he has produced life. What he means by 'life' is indicated only by his appreciating it in aesthetic terms; it is beautiful, exquisite, a work of art or a work of nature as beautiful as art. In *The Ambassadors* and many other novels, James arranges to bring aesthetic values and moral values into a pronounced degree of tension. They are different, and each set of values makes a high claim for itself. Indeed, 'life' is a value in James's novels – think of *The Tragic Muse* – only to the degree to which it admits an aesthetic consideration and lives up to it. As James remarks in the Preface to that novel:

A picture without composition slights its most precious chance for beauty, and is moreover not composed at all unless the painter knows *how* that principle of health and safety, working as an absolutely premeditated art, has prevailed. There may in its absence be life, incontestably, as 'The Newcomes' has life, as 'Les Trois Mousquetaires', as Tolstoi's 'Peace and War' have it. . . . There is life and life, and as waste is only life sacrificed and therefore prevented from 'counting', I delight in a deep-breathing economy and an organic form.[23]

So if Sir Claude has produced life in Maisie, we know what the claim amounts to only because it is followed up by the aesthetic terms which guarantee it and make it significant. In the end, according to my sense of *What Maisie Knew*, Maisie's decision brings together her moral sense and the something still deeper than a moral sense, and shows that, different as they are, they are compatible, if only in the end. The moral sense has not overwhelmed the something deeper; nor has that displaced the other. To propose, as an analogy, the tension between the moral and the aesthetic senses is only a way of putting the case.

I quote at last Miller's questions:

> Just how is the reader to evaluate Maisie's act? Is it ethically admirable? Should we try to emulate it in our own life? What would it mean to do that?[24]

I don't quite see how, even in a most serious reading of the novel, these questions arise. Miller is evidently asserting that an ethics of reading should replace an aesthetic of reading. I don't understand why. *What Maisie Knew* is a sequence of words, implying among many other things an imaginary sequence of acts and sufferances. Readers are certainly invited to participate in these sequences and to imagine their ramification; but not further to obey the narrator or the author. To take the novel as an ethical *casus* and to pursue it as such, as a case in casuistry, is to read it omnivorously. I would be willing to read the *New Testament* in that spirit, and to argue the parable of the sower and the fate of the seeds he sows, but that is because the words issue, I believe, from Christ, and have meaning upon his authority. We are not dealing with Henry James and his fictions. When we are, as in reading *What Maisie Knew*, the fiction exists in its virtuality; it is removed from existence so that it can be offered for perception alone. The book exists for perception, not for obedience or disobedience. Miller is perhaps taking literally Matthew Arnold's notion that when we have abandoned religious belief, we may still be saved by great literature. It is not true.

NOTES

1 Henry James, *The Art of Fiction and Other Essays*, with an introduction by Morris Roberts (New York: Oxford University Press, 1948), p. 59.

2 Giovanni Gentile, *The Reform of Education*, tr. Dino Bigongiari (New York: Harcourt, Brace and Co., 1922), pp. 228–9. Cf. Donald T. Torchiana, ' "Among School Children" and the Education of the Irish Spirit', in *In Excited Reverie*, eds A. N. Jeffares and K. G. W. Cross (New York: St Martin's Press), pp. 123ff.

3 *The Collected Poems of W. B. Yeats*, ed. Richard J. Finneran (New York: Macmillan Publishing Co., 1989), p. 217. Subsequent references to poems by Yeats from this edition.

4 John Hollander, *Melodious Guile: Fictive Pattern in Poetic Language* (New Haven: Yale University Press, 1988), p. 37.

5 Francis Bacon, *Essays on the Advancement of Learning, New Atlantis and Other Pieces*, ed. Richard Foster Jones (New York: Odyssey Press, 1937), p. 391.

6 Immanuel Kant, *Critique of Aesthetic Judgement*, tr. James Creed Meredith (Oxford: Clarendon Press, 1911), pp. 175–6.

7 Jean François Lyotard, *The Lyotard Reader*, ed. Andrew Benjamin (Oxford: Basil Blackwell, 1989), p. 159.

8   John Gage, *Goethe on Art* (Berkeley: University of California Press, 1980), p. 97.

9   Emmanuel Levinas, *Time and the Other*, tr. Richard A. Cohen (Pittsburgh: Duquesne University Press, 1987), pp. 124–5.

10 Emmanuel Levinas, *Totality and Infinity*, tr. Alphonso Lingis (Pittsburgh: Duquesne University Press, 1969), pp. 56, 58.

11 Susanne K. Langer, *Feeling and Form* (London: Routledge and Kegan Paul, 1953), p. 107.

12 Elizabeth Sewell, *Paul Valéry : The Mind in the Mirror* (New Haven: Yale University Press, 1952), p. 36.

13 Herbert Marcuse, *The Aesthetic Dimension: Toward a Critique of Marxist Aesthetics*, tr. Herbert Marcuse and Erica Sherover (London: Macmillan, 1979), pp. ixff.

14 Michel de Certeau, *Heterologies: Discourse and the Other*, tr. Brian Massumi (Manchester: Manchester University Press, 1986), p. 31.

15 Samuel Beckett, *Watt* (Paris: Olympia Press, 1953), pp. 30–1.

16 Philip Larkin, *High Windows* (New York: Farrar, Straus & Giroux, 1974), p. 17.

17 Henry James, *The Art of the Novel: Critical Prefaces* (Boston: Northeastern University Press, 1984), p. 142.

18 Ibid., pp. 222–3.

19 Henry James, *What Maisie Knew*, ed. Leon Edel (London: Bodley Head, 1969), p. 216.

20 Ibid., p. 276.

21 Ibid., pp. 276–7.

22 Ibid., p. 278.

23 James, *The Art of the Novel*, p. 84.

24 J. Hillis Miller, *Versions of Pygmalion* (Cambridge, Mass.: Harvard University Press, 1990), p. 39.

Being Among Words: An Interview with Denis Donoghue

FLETCHER I'd like to start off with an Irish question. In your collection of essays entitled *We Irish*, you speak of some of the particular difficulties of being an Irish writer, difficulties that were felt and expressed most cogently, perhaps, by James Joyce, whom you quote. You say of Irish writers that 'they cannot be completely at ease with their acquired speech' and that, 'like Stephen, the Irish writer speaks and writes in English but with resentment, fretful in its shadow'. I think I understand the political and historical reasons for that feeling, and yet I want to take issue with you a little on this point. From the English side, we see Irish writers using the language with consummate skill, exploiting its beauty and richness, inventing it, if you will. Indeed, if there's one hoary cliché about the Irish that everyone knows, it's that they have the gift of the gab. You yourself write effortless and delightful prose, so I'd like to ask whether you personally feel that English is an acquired speech? Are you fretful in its shadow?

DONOGHUE What I had in mind is that an Irish writer writes the English language with misgiving, a feeling of disloyalty. Think of Michael Hartnett, an Irish poet who wrote for many years in English, then gave it up and wrote a book called *Farewell to English* and writes now in Irish. That's an extreme case, but I'm thinking of other poets who feel that they have a responsibility to the Irish language: Seamus Heaney, for instance, and Thomas Kinsella. This partly accounts for the provenance of translation, as in Heaney's *Sweeney Astray* and Kinsella's *Táin*. These books, apart from their intrinsic interest, are expressions of loyalty towards a defeated language. Irish didn't fail; it was suppressed. During what we call the years of the Penal Laws, it was a crime to speak Irish. The defeat of the language was accomplished by the eighteenth century. But the eighteenth century isn't all that long ago, and many Irish writers feel something of what Joyce assigned to Stephen Dedalus, a sense that he is speaking the language of the conqueror. This sense was part of Stephen's resentment. I'm not sure that Joyce as a historical person felt it. At least, I don't recall any evidence in his letters and so on that he felt resentful about using the English language.

FLETCHER   Do you think it's possible that the resentment you speak of fuels the energy with which Irish writers use the language?

DONOGHUE   It may do, because it italicizes certain emotions and passions. Since violence broke out again in the north of Ireland in 1968, we are all much more self-conscious about language, and literature has become more tendentious; the debate about literature in Ireland has become more polemical. So it could be that that resentment has brought forth or exacerbated certain qualities in Irish writing. But the relation between the English language and the Irish writer is more complicated than that. You mentioned the gift of the gab. There is a long tradition of the stage Irishman who goes to England and woos English audiences with that gift. That, too, is politically contentious.

FLETCHER   Would there be a parallel with, say, Third World writers who use English today?

DONOGHUE   Yes. Using English, they participate in a
world situation which is dominated by England and America, or rather by America; they've made a concession right
from the beginning. I don't think they've sold their birth-
right or their soul, and I don't even feel this about Irish
writers. Indeed, there may well be Irish writers who don't
feel any resentment about English. But most of the Irish
writers known to me have some sense of a differentness
that has to be reckoned with. John Montague, for example,
and Tom Paulin. These writers are not just genially aware
of being Irish; they are sensitive to the intimate, linguistic
question, the politics of language.

FLETCHER   A question about values: you've always
been concerned with questions of value, it seems to me; in
writing about Yeats's poetry you say that it poses the
question: 'In a world of mutability, what remains? What
is possible? Where does value reside?' And you give the
answer for Yeats: 'The answer, but not the whole story, is
in the imagination of man.' Wouldn't you say that the same
question, and perhaps the same answer, haunts your own
criticism?

DONOGHUE   I've been trying to find some way of reading literature, bearing in mind the fundamental fact that it
is literature. This is contentious these days. Suppose, for
example, one were to quote Eliot's remark that if you read
literature, it is as literature you must read it and not as
another thing. That would now be deemed either foolish
or tautological; people would say, well, what do you mean
by literature as literature? If you try to set up literature as
a category or a mode of life, a way of being present in the
world, you're immediately accused of being totalitarian.
Literature is different from either a conversation or a discourse; it's a question of trying to see what the difference
amounts to. That's why I think the issue of form is inescap-
able, and why I would now take any risk involved in being

a formalist. We must somehow say what form means. That's why I value Marcuse's insistence on the formal value of art, that it is in its form that literature is revolutionary, not in its content. It is in its content having become form or having fulfilled itself as form. Unless we can recognize a work of art as form, we haven't recognized it at all. The difficulty then would be how to answer someone who would say that in talking about form I'm trying to put up a rampart and to make of a poem a well-wrought urn. But it seems to me that we could capitalize upon the very impurity of our words. I think Valéry made this comment in relation to the word 'light'; in literature it's a word with great reverberation, but equally someone can walk up to another on the street, hold out a cigarette, and say, 'Can you give me a light?' It's a mundane word; but equally it's a word that can be used in rarified senses. One of the difficulties of literature is that the words poets use are simultaneously mundane and esoteric. Their first character is to be mundane, and yet a writer will try to alter the character of a word by setting it in a new network of relations.

FLETCHER So is that the imagination at work, producing form?

DONOGHUE I think that's where the imagination comes in. The imagination can indeed take perfectly ordinary materials, ordinary words we hear in the street, but can somehow alter them by a flick of feeling or a flick of relation which will somehow give them new values and new propensities. I wouldn't want to disavow the ordinariness either of the ordinary universe or of ordinary language. It's the same materials all along the line. Even a poet as esoteric as Wallace Stevens is still for the most part using standard words, but he's using them in the midst of cadences, echoes, recesses, and reverberations, putting them in new contexts, so that the consequence is indeed a poetic act. I

can't see how we could do without the word 'imagination'.
It is mischievous to claim that talk of imagination is self-
bewilderment or mystification. There is a difference
between someone who is an artist and someone who isn't.
In the eyes of God there may be no difference, but in
quotidian eyes there has to be a difference. Some people
are gifted in that way. You have only to stand in front of
a great painting to realize that some people are geniuses
and other people aren't. I feel bound to retain the whole
Romantic vocabulary – imagination, genius, and so forth.

SCHWEIZER In *The Sovereign Ghost* you claim that
imagination is 'a genuine ability', and you ask that, 'if we
cannot account for it, we should confess our failure, rather
than assert that it is unaccountable'. What really is the
difference between these two responses, or to say this
differently, how do I know that imagination is not accountable if I fail to account for it?

DONOGHUE My Reith Lectures were called *The Arts
Without Mystery*, and that title was ironic, because I think
that the arts without mystery are inconceivable, and I want
to retain the mystery. To take a case in point: if for the
hundredth time I read *The Waste Land*, I still feel that it
is a work of genius, unaccountable in the sense that no
considerations fully account for it. There are things we can
say about it, but there is a final sense that it is what it is and
cannot become entirely transparent to us. 'Accountable' is
perhaps the wrong word. I think all I really meant there
was to respect the palpable existence of a faculty which is
indeed creative and quite extraordinary and not to be
reduced, as structuralists used to tell us, to a system of
codes. No system of codes produced *The Waste Land*, even
though Eliot resorted to many systems, anthropological,
religious, allusive, cultural, and so on. I'm not in any way
suggesting that the work arose out of thin air: it's a poem
extraordinarily dense with historical and cultural forma-

tions, but the sense of life, the sense of language which took that particular form is not to be explained, much less explained away.

SCHWEIZER But why is it then that we fail to recognize the imagination?

DONOGHUE I don't want to be too stringent about this, but we are living at a time when there is an ambition on the part of many people for total explanation. This is partly a matter of positivism; it's partly the Enlightenment project and a feeling of disgust occasioned by anything that seems to resist final explanation. I don't share this ambition. Nor does it trouble me when we have to say that the rest is silence. I don't feel resentful when Eliot in *Four Quartets* points beyond what can be known and said to what can't. Some readers are irritated by this. Leavis was wrong to say, about the Chinese jar in *Four Quartets*, that when Eliot appeals to the notion of form or the still point of the turning world or the Chinese jar he's making a claim to know the reality behind these notations. I don't think Eliot is making a claim to know anything. He's positing a limit beyond which it is impossible to know. One of the difficulties we face as teachers of literature is that scientific explanation and technology hold out to people the promise that total knowledge and total possession of nature are indeed possible. Our students are very resistant to the notion that there are forms of language which gesture beyond themselves.

FLETCHER I'm still trying, in a sense, to place you as a critic. You said you're almost prepared to call yourself a formalist, and you've acknowledged a debt to various American critics who were formalists; but I wonder whether you don't also owe something to another tradition, an English moral tradition that goes, say, from Samuel Johnson through Arnold to Leavis?

DONOGHUE   That's true. But I would like to acknowledge that moral emphasis by almost endlessly postponing its application. When I think of myself in some relation to aesthetic or formal experience, I still don't regard a work of literature as a free-floating object or as having no relation to historical, cultural, economic, and political considerations. Of course it does. But the difficulty, the point of embarrassment in the moral tradition, is precisely the point at which the moral decision is taken. The decision has to be taken, but I want to keep postponing it. There's nothing wrong with the moral emphasis unless it is premature, applied before it has to be.

FLETCHER   Do you feel this happens in Eliot's later criticism, for example?

DONOGHUE   Yes, I do. In *After Strange Gods*, Eliot brings down the axe far too quickly. The animus which he directs in *After Strange Gods* against Hardy, Lawrence, and Yeats, the way in which in that book he exempts only Joyce, and Joyce only in terms of his ethical orthodoxy – that strikes me as premature. If Eliot had done an elaborate analysis of the fictions he refers to, he might still have pronounced upon the strain of cruelty he found in modern fiction. But, without the analysis, the moral decision is merely an assertion. He was, as he said himself, a sick soul when he wrote that book, and I certainly wouldn't hold him to account. But he felt, from 1927 on, that literary criticism should not be merely literary; it should be completed by a criticism in moral terms.

FLETCHER   You've said, also about Arnold, that it's chiefly because of Arnold that literary criticism has not become, to its own impoverishment, entirely literary, which seems to work a little bit in the other direction. The kind of general criticism that Arnold practised I think you practise as well, but there aren't many people who do that nowadays.

DONOGHUE   I think of myself as a generalist, rather than a specialist. But there's a great temptation in being a generalist; one gets into the habit of merely using literature as exemplification, and I think Arnold did that. When he quotes a few lines from Chaucer or Dante, it's always with an exemplifying motive. I don't want to talk about literature as chiefly exemplifying something that's going on in society. I want to give literature more space to move in, and not to be pressing upon it to disclose its character.

FLETCHER   Would you say, then, that in a sense we're exploiting literature?

DONOGHUE   Yes. Most of the exploitation is being done by the ideologically insistent critics. Like Eliot, they bring in the verdict too soon. I think it's unfortunate that Fredric Jameson, for instance, has criticized the early Joyce and the early Eliot for making available to people what he calls 'strategies of inwardness' to deal with an alienated universe. I see nothing sinister in introspection or in the soliloquy or in privacy; but I can see why Jameson takes that view, that clearly he wants people, in an unhappy world, simply to go out and change the world – or at least, that's what he seems to be proposing. But where that has the effect of banning inwardness and the kind of internal brooding and rumination which we find in a Stephen Dedalus or Prufrock, that seems to me totalitarian in its way. It's a strikingly illiberal position for a self-proclaimed liberal to take.

SCHWEIZER   Maybe, then, deconstruction is a strategy against that totalitarian impatience, because of its advocacy of deferral and its critique of certainty and judgement.

DONOGHUE   My only qualification of that is that I wish I could be more convinced that deconstructionists really do want to get back into literature. I would be very happy with literary theory if it were prolegomena to enable us to arrive at sustainable but not congealed positions and to enable us then to be better readers – which is, after all, what Richards and Empson were really trying to do. But I don't believe that it is doing that. I think one of the troubles is that literary theory, precisely because it has become an activity in its own right, has then claimed and practised a degree of autonomy, and it no longer sees itself in any vivid relation to literature. I'm unreconstructed enough to think that the only good reason for having an interest in theory is that it might, much later in the day, make one a better, more responsive, more scrupulous reader. It's entirely possible that, if a student were to carefully read, say, the work of Paul de Man, he or she might indeed become a better reader of poetry. But I think, in common practice, the effort of reading these extremely difficult and arduous works comes to take the place of a reading of literature.

SCHWEIZER   You quote Derrida in *The Sovereign Ghost*, and it seems to me that, subsequently, your critique of deconstruction becomes more and more hostile. I wonder why, since you yourself seem to make use of many of its insights, precisely, for example, in your notion of the postponement or deferment of the moral decision and of the critical judgement.

DONOGHUE   My relation to deconstruction for a time was indeed hostile, but has in fact become much less so. What I've written about Derrida, Paul de Man, and others in the last few years is much more appreciative than earlier stuff I published. I saw nothing in deconstruction but vanity flaunting itself as scruple. An early article of mine in the *New York Review of Books* was very hostile. I wouldn't write in that spirit now. But I would suggest a difference in our various modes of deferment and post-ponement. The reason I want to postpone a critical judgement is that I think the moral consideration is humiliated by any premature application. I would feel justified in proposing a moral judgement on a work of art, but only after I had given it considerable latitude in its own terms, whatever they are. The situation has changed from the time when Eliot said that the function of criticism is the elucidation of works of art and the correction of taste. It is still feasible to say that criticism is the elucidation of works of art, but how would you even go about correcting taste? What is the taste to be corrected? How could we appeal to it? If I wanted to separate myself from the deconstructionists, I would say that there is a kind of shadow, a dark consideration which is moral, indeed ethical, and which demands to be acknowledged; but I would always be saying, yes, but not just yet. There will be time. My criticism is becoming more ethical and at the same time more respectful of form, more sensitive to the antinomian claim of form. The real difficulty is how to bring those two recognitions together. This is why I'm quoting Levinas; I think the ethical emphasis is fundamental. I think our terms of reference ought to be ethics and justice. The problem, then, is how to embody those judgements in forms which are not vulgar and premature, how to reconcile those judgements with a formal emphasis. The only way I could see to do that would be somehow to regard the achievement of form as simultaneously an ethical and an aesthetic achievement. It's difficult; these are intangible matters.

SCHWEIZER So you would articulate your own interest in ethics, at this time, differently, say, from Hillis Miller's *Ethics of Reading*?

DONOGHUE Yes. I've argued with Hillis Miller a little about *The Ethics of Reading*. I would use the word 'ethics' in a far more fundamental way. I respect the way in which Miller uses the word 'ethics'. He means the kind of ethical inclination or decision which is represented by writing a footnote to one's own work, that you qualify something you've just written. For him, ethics is a second thought brought to bear upon a first. My ethical emphasis – and this is where Levinas keeps coming into it – is primordial. It is not a footnote to the text. It is the text, in so far as it has achieved itself under ethical impulsion or ethical recognition. What I'm trying to do is to posit the ethical as the primordial and to see its trajectory culminating in an achieved form, and that form in no way diminished by its being form and its calling for consideration in formal terms. The part of contemporary rhetoric that I want to resist is the tendency to make form ashamed of itself, or to make those who talk about form ashamed of themselves. I have the same feeling about a word even more difficult to rehabilitate, the word 'aesthete'. It seems nearly impossible to recuperate the word 'aesthete', and it would be interesting to trace the process by which that word was diminished. When Yeats wrote about the tragic generation, what was mainly tragic about those writers was not their biographical collapse into drink and dissipation, but that they felt it impossible to participate in a common life. Yeats says that many English writers leaned upon a common life, participated in it, and gained sustenance from it. But in the late nineteenth century, conditions became such that certain writers, including himself, Lionel Johnson, Symons, Dowson, and several others, felt that they could not do this, and therefore that they must propose what Yeats calls 'images separated from the general purposes of human life', and he says of these images that 'they grow in beauty as they grow in sterility'. That's a very questionable phrase. By definition, sterility is what cannot grow; but you can see what Yeats means, that these images achieve a kind of vulnerable and appalled beauty, precisely to the degree to which they have to exist in some mode other than that of common life.

SCHWEIZER You write at the end of *Ferocious Alphabets*, where you reassess Stevens, that 'his category, his way of being in the world, is not knowledge but pleasure'. You also write, however, that Derrida's notion of play implies 'an air of triviality'. Is Stevens's pleasure more laudable, less trivial than Derrida's?

DONOGHUE What I resented at that stage in Derrida was that he was taking a perfectly valid and very serious terminology, Schiller's terminology of play, and I thought he was trivializing it. I'm thinking of *Glas* and Derrida's breaking up of words and putting brackets around certain syllables and so on. I cannot believe that that is what Schiller had in mind when he was talking about play. I think I was resenting the kidnapping of the vocabulary of play. Derrida doesn't do that always. For example, in 'Structure, Sign, and Play', it seems to me, he's still using that term in a thoroughly Schillerean and valid way. The distinction he makes in that essay is very useful and one that could be developed. The notion of play is important but questionable, in the sense that it could go either way. It could become, in a Schillerean tradition, a serious activity and a creative one; but equally you could tip it over into mere lexical fiddling. I felt that in *Glas* Derrida was doing that. In regard to Stevens and pleasure, I was there reacting against some of my own early essays where I was taking Stevens very seriously as a philosophic poet in the tradition from Lucretius to Wordsworth and Goethe. I was trying to find in Stevens's poetry a consistent philosophic position. At a certain point I gave that up – there was no consistency – and I started thinking that he was a moody poet and that this was one of the marvellous things about him. There are moods in Stevens which represent virtually the whole spectrum of possibility, and then there are poems which go along with these. I still think that one of the good aims of criticism is to rehabilitate the notion of pleasure in an entirely untrivial way, but it's very difficult because literature has to such an extent been harnessed to ideological purposes; it's almost as difficult to talk about the pleasures of reading as it is to talk about an aesthetic experience. I'm aware that Robert Alter has written a fine book called *The Pleasure of Reading*, but I think we've reached a rather harsh situation – that is, some critics love literature and some resent it. Some write about literature in a way that testifies to an irrefutable love of being amongst words, and other critics write about literature with suspicion and resentment. But what seems to be worth saying is that we can read Stevens and other poets, giving them their day in court, allowing them the range of their moods, not forcing them to be strict philosophers or to step into some line of coherence, and we can respond to their different moods as human possibilities. That's, I think, what it comes back to. The only real justification for literature is that it provides us with ways of imagining what it would be like to be different. That's the basis of sympathies and recognitions. You could say, of course, can't we be sympathetic simply by virtue of the fact that we are human, that we are born and that we will die. But that is too abstract. One of the great things about literature is that the different moods and recognitions are given a kind of notional validity in the poems. The mood in which Stevens writes 'The Course of a Particular' is not a stern, decisive, philosophic position that he would be prepared to live by. It is occasional. The fact that that poem is perhaps his finest single work, as I believe it is, arises from the dignity and the nobility of his being in that way among the words. Now the pleasure of the poem is certainly the pleasure of recognition; it's the pleasure of participating in feelings and moods not one's own.

FLETCHER   I'd like to suggest that in certain respects, you consistently go against the grain; that you have, if you like, your own brand of nonconformism. You were reading

American literature at a time when it was hardly fashionable or even respectable to do so on the other side of the Atlantic. While your colleagues were reading Leavis and *Scrutiny*, you had turned to the American New Critics. You have continued to write about Yeats, even though he has come under attack in Ireland, and now you have embarked on a project to rescue literature from theory. Do you see yourself as a fighter for unpopular causes, at all?

DONOGHUE Not really. It's not so much that I want to rescue literature from theory. I want to redefine theory. I would like to see theory becoming much more speculative, much more experimental. I'd like to see it being written in much the way in which many poems are written, as an exploration among the possibilities of words. I don't want theory to be a function of an already determined politics. I would also want it to respect terms and values which are under great pressure. I've mentioned some of them already: 'pleasure', 'aesthetics', 'form'. But I want these terms to be shadowed by more sullen ones, terms which exert pressure upon them. I wouldn't like to be able to use the word 'pleasure' in a self-satisfied, complacent way, as if I had easy access to it.

SCHWEIZER Speaking of unpopular causes and going against the grain, *Warrenpoint* seems to me to pay a curiously un-Freudian, un-oedipal tribute to your father. Is *Warrenpoint* a conscious refutation of Freud? I remember that you say that Freud has caused much mischief in families, setting sons against fathers. You do make use of Freud throughout your work, but this book is very un-Freudian in the sense that your degree of identification with your father is indeed very unusual.

DONOGHUE It is a very un-Freudian book. Much as I respect – indeed, revere – Freud, I think he did a lot of damage in one respect. He promulgated one story and one story only; he gave privilege to the notion that the only way in which the son can develop is by slaying the father and making space for himself. Freud did a good deal of damage even in literary criticism, in the sense that he gives the will only one thing to do. I've often had this dispute with Harold Bloom; I haven't any objection to his identifying imagination and will. My objection is to the Freudian emphasis that he gives the will; once he has posited the imagination as being identical with the will, he gives the will only one thing to do; it has only one story to tell, one drama to enact, and that is the slaying of the father. Again, Levinas is very much to the point, because Levinas, too, emphasizes the will, but he gives it a far greater range of activities in the world and, above all, he values the will in its act of self-abnegation in favour of other people. There is no provision for that act, which I regard as ethically the noblest act available to us, either in Freud or in Bloom. In Bloom all the will can do is maintain itself against every object in experience. This seems to me an appalling constriction. I would want to give the will far greater latitude of choices, rather than the one embodied in slaying the father. Bloom represents this in relation to the Satan of *Paradise Lost*. He regards Satan's self-invention and self-creation as the most profound act that can be performed. I regard the Satan of *Paradise Lost* as a spoiled brat. I see no nobility whatever in the claim to self-creation. I regard it as mostly disgusting. Levinas is on stronger ground and also far more humane in holding out the possibility that the will would exert itself in an entirely different mode and in an entirely different style and based upon quite a different range of recognitions. I think that the consequences of Bloom's criticism are seriously misleading. It is absurd that, following Freud, he regards writers as divisible into strong poets and weak poets. A strong poet is one who sees himself in Freudian terms and establishes a Freudian relation with his precursor. Blake's relation to Milton would seem to fit into that category, and there are many others. Norman Mailer's relation to Hemingway is a case in point, where the predominant relation is one of wrestling, aggression, and so on. But to represent Eliot's relation to Dante or to Virgil or to Goethe as testifying to Eliot's being a weak poet seems to me nonsense. The relation between Eliot and Dante is a sustaining one. Eliot gains strength from Dante without feeling that he has to take Dante on, or that he has to wrestle him to the ground. Bloom damagingly limits what the will can choose to do.

FLETCHER Feminists have made the same complaint about Bloom. They see the relationships between women writers and their precursors, if one wants to use Bloom's term, in very different ways, in non-Freudian ways. I don't suppose you find yourself in too much agreement with feminist critics, but you might agree with them on this issue.

DONOGHUE The only way in which I find myself in disagreement with certain feminists is that they have not been willing to maintain any sense of discrimination. That's one of the ways in which the ideological emphasis has been seriously damaging. When I am invited by the editors of *The Norton Anthology of Literature by Women* to take an interest in the fiction of Edna O'Brien merely because she is a woman, that seems to me an inadequate reason.

SCHWEIZER We wanted to close with a question that might perhaps be unanswerable. In *The Arts Without Mystery* you insist that 'the arts are no substitute for religion', that 'there is nothing in art or in our sense of art which corresponds to my belief in God. In art, faith does not arise.' But in the same argument you also quote Northrop Frye as saying that 'perhaps it is only through the study of works of human imagination that we can make any real contact with the level of vision beyond faith'. My question is this: Is art, when it harbours something irreducibly mysterious then not a spiritual prelude, so to speak, to a greater mystery? You do speak, in *Ferocious Alphabets*, for example, of the sacredness, the mystery of poetry.

DONOGHUE I would be suspicious of any attempt to approach religious conviction by way of an engagement with art. One's relation to religious belief is indeed a matter of one's upbringing, of living within a particular tradition. I would probably not be a Catholic but for the fact that I was born and brought up in a Catholic family in Ireland. My own view thereafter is that a religious conviction is really almost primordial, in the sense that it is not achieved through something else. It is given or produced. I would wonder about a religious conviction approached through aesthetic experiences. An aesthetic experience should not be valued for leading to something else; it is an intrinsic event and should be valued as an act of perception.

FLETCHER You don't think it might have a spiritual dimension even though it lacks any doctrinal conviction?

DONOGHUE It might have; but then I would worry about the value to be attached to 'spiritual' in that sense. My relation to religion is doctrinal and dogmatic. I don't value my religious belief for the emotions it gives me, but because it enables me to believe in something I have not invented, something that is independent of me. I acknowledge the doctrines of the Catholic Church because I believe them to be true. It is not because I feel good in their presence, or because they give me a further range of emotions. That's not of any interest at all. I would be somewhat suspicious about any approach to a form of spirituality through art or literature or music, in which I was under no obligation to believe anything. I would want to believe first, and then let that incorporate whatever we mean by spirituality.

SCHWEIZER Nevertheless, your very notion of the mystery of art seems to have spiritual dimensions . . .

DONOGHUE It's not a religious mystery in the sense in which the very existence of the world is a mystery. I don't know why the world exists. The fact that it exists seems to me mysterious and a refutation of paganism. But when we talk about the spirituality of art or the spirituality of an aesthetic experience, I'd ask, what exactly is this spirituality? Is it just another emotion, or a vague sense of the numinous, or what? I suspect those words which seem to participate in a religious vocabulary but without being committed to anything. Religion is a matter of belief in the first instance. Then, indeed, it becomes a matter of practice and morality; and there I fail just as everyone fails, and perhaps more grievously. But fundamentally it is a matter of belief. Eliot said that what really matters is sin and redemption. I believe that to be true. That's why I'm uncomfortable with the vocabulary of spirituality; it seems to me just a psychological vocabulary having to do with certain emotions rather than others.

Denis Donoghue: A Bibliography, 1954–1991
Compiled by Chris Bittenbender and Richard Kahn

1954

1 'Macklin's "Shylock and Macbeth"', *Studies* 43 (Winter), pp. 421–30.
2 Review of *The Identity of Yeats* by Richard Ellmann, *Studies* 43 (Winter), pp. 482–4.

1955

3 'The Bird as Symbol: Hopkins's "Windhover"', *Studies* 44 (Autumn), pp. 291–9.
4 'The Critic in Reaction: Lionel Trilling', *Twentieth Century* 158 (October), pp. 376–83.
5 'Notes towards a Critical Method: Language as Order', *Studies* 44 (Summer), pp. 181–92.
6 'Reflections of an English Writer in Ireland: D. Davie', *Studies* 44 (Winter), pp. 439–45.
7 'Synge's *Riders to the Sea*: a Study', *University Review* 1 (Summer), pp. 52–8.
8 'Synge's *The Tinker's Wedding*: a Study', *Irish Writing* 30 (March), pp. 56–62.
9 'Technique in Hopkins', *Studies* 44 (Winter), pp. 446–56.
10 'Mummy Truths to Tell', *Irish Times* 30577, p. 6 (Review of *W. B. Yeats: A Special Number*, *Irish Writing* 31).

1956

11 'Poetry and the New Conservatism', *London Magazine* 3, no. 4 (April), pp. 54–63.
12 'Reading a Poem; Empson's *"Arachne"*', *Studies* 45 (Summer), pp. 216–26. Reprinted in *England, Their England* (1988), pp. 299–305.

1957

13 'Flowers and Timber: A Note on Synge's Poems', *Threshold* 1 (Autumn), pp. 40–7.
14 'Irish Writing', *The Month* 17 (March), pp. 180–5.
15 'Joyce's Psychological Landscapes', *Studies* 46 (Spring), pp. 76–90.
16 'Poetic in the Common Enterprise', *Twentieth Century* 161 (June), pp. 537–45 (correction in vol. 162, p. 78).
17 'Yeats and the Clean Outline', *Sewanee Review* 65, no. 2 (Spring), pp. 202–25. Reprinted in *The Third Voice* (1959), pp. 32–61.

1958

18 'For a Redeeming Language: William Carlos Williams in American Literature', *Twentieth Century* 162 (June), pp. 532–42. Reprinted in *William Carlos Williams: A Collection of Critical Essays*, ed. J. Hillis Miller (Englewood Cliffs, N.J.: Prentice-Hall, 1966), pp. 121–31. Reprinted in *The Ordinary Universe (1968)*, pp. 180–93. Also reprinted in *William Carlos Williams*, ed. Charles Tomlinson (London: Penguin, 1972), pp. 383–8.
19 'Irische Literatur nach Yeats und Joyce', *Dokumente* 14, no. 3 (June), pp. 233–5.
20 'Shakespeare's Rhetoric', *Studies* 47 (Winter), pp. 431–40. Reprinted in *England, Their England* (1988), pp. 37–48.
21 'Theatre Poetry and Dramatic Verse', *Studies* 47 (Autumn), pp. 305–23. Reprinted in *The Third Voice* (1959), pp. 243–76.

22 'Since our Concern was Speech', *Sewanee Review* 67, no. 1 (Winter), pp. 117–22 (Review of *Modern Verse in English 1900–1950*, ed. David Cecil and Allen Tate).

1959

23 *The Third Voice: Modern British and American Verse Drama* (Princeton, N.J.: Princeton University Press), 288 pp.
24 'Christopher Fry's Theatre of Words', *Essays in Criticism* 9, no. 1 (January), pp. 37–49. Reprinted in *The Third Voice*, pp.180–92.
25 'Eliot in Fair Colonus', *Studies* 48 (Spring), pp. 49–58.
26 'The Limitations of Robert Frost', *Twentieth Century* 166 (July), pp. 13–22.
27 'The Vigour of its Blood: Yeats's "Words for Music Perhaps"', *Kenyon Review* 21, no. 3 (Summer), pp. 376–87.
28 Review of *Prolegomena to the Study of Yeats's Poems* by George B. Saul, *Studies 48* (Spring), pp. 106–8.

1960

29 (Ed.) *The Permanence of Yeats* (The Thomas Davis Lectures, broadcast by Radio Eireann, September).
30 'Dublin Letter', *Hudson Review* 13 (Winter), pp. 579–85.
31 'Joyce and the Finite Order', *Sewanee Review* 68, no. 2 (Spring), pp. 256–73.
32 'Wallace Stevens and the Abstract Order', *Studies* 49 (Winter), pp. 389–406.
33 'Eliot in the Sibyl's Leaves', *Sewanee Review* 68, no. 1 (Winter), pp. 138–43 (Review of *The Invisible Poet: T. S. Eliot* by Hugh Kenner).
34 'For Civility: an Emersonian Ideal', *Poetry* 96, no. 6 (September), pp. 382–7 (Review of *Emerson: A Modern Anthology*, eds Alfred Kazin and Daniel Aaron, and other recent publications).
35 'Off-Centre', *Kenyon Review* 21, no. 4, pp. 644–7 (Review of *Vision and Rhetoric* by G. S. Fraser).

1961

36 'The Human Image in Yeats', *London Magazine* 1, no. 9 (December), pp. 51–65.

37 'In the Scene of Being', *Hudson Review* 14, no. 2 (Summer), pp. 232–46.

38 'London Letter: Moral West End', *Hudson Review* 14, no. 1 (Spring), pp. 93–103.

39 'Poetry and the Behavior of Speech', *Hudson Review* 14, no. 4 (Winter), pp. 537–49.

40 'Songs the Sirens Sing', *Studies* 50 (Winter), pp. 403–14.

41 'Tradition, Poetry and W. B. Yeats', *Sewanee Review* 69, no. 3, pp. 476–84. (Review of *Tradition and Poetic Structure* by J. V. Cunningham and *The Poetry of W. B. Yeats* by Yvor Winters).

1962

42 'T. S. Eliot's *The Cocktail Party*', in *T. S. Eliot: A Collection of Critical Essays*, ed. Hugh Kenner, pp. 173–86 (Abridged from *The Third Voice*, 1959).

43 'After Reading Hannah Arendt', *Poetry* 100 (May), pp. 127–30.

44 'A Mode of Communication: Robert Frost and the Middle Style', *Yale Review* 52 (December), pp. 205–19.

45 'The Play of Words', *Listener* 68, no. 1737 (12 July), pp. 55–7.

46 'Dear Shadows', *Nation* 195, no. 10, pp. 203–4 (Review of *Dublin in the Age of William Butler Yeats and James Joyce* by Richard Morgan Kain).

47 'God on Chevauchee', *Hudson Review* 15 (Spring), pp. 154–60 (Review of *Religion in Modern English Drama* by Gerald Weakes).

1963

48 'Hibernus Ludens', *Hudson Review* 16 (Autumn), pp. 450–4.

49 'A Note on Swift', *New Statesman* 66 (December 13),
    pp. 877–8.

50 'The Sacred Rage: Three American Poets', *Listener* 69, no.
    1784 (6 June), pp. 965–7.

51 'The Values of *Moll Flanders*', *Sewanee Review* 71, no. 2
    (Spring), pp. 287–303. Reprinted in *Daniel Defoe: Schriften
    zum Erzählwerk* (1982), pp. 126–41. Also reprinted in
    England, Their England (1988), pp. 64–78.

52 'Countries of the Mind', *Guardian* 36241 (6 January), p. 5
    (Review of *The Yeats Country* by Sheelah Kirby, *William
    Morris and W. B. Yeats* by Peter Faulkner, and *Yeats the
    Playwright* by Peter Ure).

53 'Impassioned Clay', *Hudson Review* 16 (Winter), p. 617
    (Review of *John Keats* by Aileen Ward and *John Keats* by
    Walter Jackson Bates).

1964

54 (Ed.), *The Integrity of Yeats* (Cork: Mercier Press), 70 pp.
    (The Thomas Davis Lectures).

55 'Yeats and Modern Poetry: An Introduction', in *The Integrity
    of Yeats*, pp. 6–20.

56 'Commitment and *The Dangling Man*', *Studies* 53 (Summer),
    pp. 174–87. Reprinted as 'Dangling Man' in *The Ordinary
    Universe* (1968), pp. 194–220.

57 'An Interview with Richard Eberhart', *Shenandoah* 15, no.
    4 (Summer), pp. 7–29.

58 'The Good Old Complex Fate', *Hudson Review* 17, no. 2
    (Spring), pp. 267–78 (Review of recently published poetry).

59 'The Well-Tempered Klavier', *Hudson Review* 17, no. 1
    (Winter), pp. 138–42 (Review of *Fables of Identity* by
    Northrop Frye).

1965

60 *Connoisseurs of Chaos: Ideas of Order in Modern American
    Poetry* (New York: Macmillan), 254 pp. Reissued in paper-
    back, 1984 (New York: Columbia University Press).

61 *Emily Dickinson: Connoisseur of Chaos.* Recording in the
    Series *Against the Sky: A Short View of American Poetry,*
    1850–1950 (Cincinnati: University of Cincinnati and
    National Association of Educational Broadcasters), one hour
    (adapted from 'Emily Dickinson', in *Connoisseurs of Chaos,*
    pp. 100–28).

62 (Ed. with J. R. Mulryne), *An Honoured Guest: New Essays*
    on W. B. Yeats (London: Edward Arnold), viii, 196 pp.

63 'Nuances of a Theme by Wallace Stevens', in *The Act of*
    Mind: Essays on the Poetry of Wallace Stevens, eds Roy
    Harvey Pearce and J. Hillis Miller (Baltimore: Johns Hop-
    kins University Press), pp. 224–42. Reprinted in *The Ordi-*
    nary Universe (1968), pp. 221–40.

64 'On "The Winding Stair"', in *An Honoured Guest,*
    pp. 106–23. Reprinted in *We Irish* (1986), pp. 67–88.

65 'Roethke's Broken Music', in *Theodore Roethke: Essays on the*
    Poetry, ed. Arnold Stein (Seattle: University of Washington
    Press), pp.136–66. Reprinted from *Connoisseurs of Chaos,*
    pp. 216–45.

66 'Melville as Poet', *Lugano Review* (Switzerland) 1, no. 1,
    pp. 67–82.

67 'Towards the Far Field: the Poetry of Theodore Roethke',
    Lugano Review (Switzerland) 1, no. 2, pp. 50–72.

68 'T. S. Eliot's Quartets: A New Reading', *Studies* 54 (Spring),
    pp. 41–62. Reprinted in *The Ordinary Universe* (1968),
    pp. 241–66.

69 'Bent Sinister', *Irish Times* 34207 (5 June) (Review of *In*
    Exciting Reverie: A Centenary Tribute to William Butler Yeats,
    eds A. N. Jeffares and K. G. W. Cross).

70 Review of *The Correspondence of Jonathan Swift,* vols. 4 and
    5, ed. Harold Williams, *New Statesman* 69 (14 May), p. 766;
    and *Times Literary Supplement* 3300 (27 May), p. 424.

71 'Dark Angels', *Manchester Guardian Weekly* (29 July), p. 11
    (Review of *White Mule* by William Carlos Williams).

72 'A Man of Words', *New York Review of Books* 5, no. 3 (26
    August), pp. 17–18 (Review of *James, Seumas and Jacques:*
    Unpublished Writings of James Stephens, ed. Lloyd Franken-
    berg and *James Stephens: His Work and an Account of His Life*
    by Hilary Pyle). Reprinted in *We Irish* (1986), pp. 204–8.

73 'The Store of the Human', *Hudson Review* 18, no. 3 (Autumn), pp. 601–7 (Review of recently published poetry).

1966

74 'Come to Dublin', *New Statesman* 72 (14 October), pp. 563–4.
75 'Conrad's Facts', *New Statesman* 72 (26 August), p. 291.
76 'The Long Poem', *New York Review of Books* 6, no. 6 (14 April), pp. 18–20.
77 'Secret Agents', *New Statesman* 72 (11 November), p. 706.
78 'Yeats and the Living Voice', *Studies* 55 (Summer), pp. 147–65. Reprinted in *The Ordinary Universe* (1968), pp. 125–45.
79 'Aboriginal Poet', *New York Review of Books* 7, No. 4 (22 September), pp. 14–16 (Review of *Collected Poems* by Theodore Roethke and *Theodore Roethke: An Introduction to the Poetry* by Karl Malkoff).
80 'Between the Lines', *Guardian* 37234 (25 March), p. 8 (Review of *Yeats's Verse Plays: The Revisions* by Suheil Badi Bushrui).
81 Review of *Jane Austen and her Predecessors* by Frank Wilson Bradbrock, *New Statesman* 71 (13 May), pp. 698–9.
82 Review of *Letters of Wallace Stevens*, selected and edited by Holly Stevens, *New York Review of Books* 7, no. 9 (1 December), p. 6.
83 'Miracle Plays', *New York Review of Books* 7, no. 6 (20 October), pp. 25–7 (Review of *Miracles*, ed. Richard Lewis, *Bertha and Other Plays* by Kenneth Koch, *Reasons of the Heart* and *Cipango's Hinder Door* by Edward Dahlberg).
84 'Penny Worlds of the Poets', *Encounter* 27 (September), pp. 69–70 (Review of *Selected Poems* by Louis Simpson).
85 'Sea of Troubles', *Hudson Review* 19, no. 4 (Winter), pp. 503–5 (Review of *Psychoanalysis and Shakespeare* by Norman Holland).

1967

86   'The Lost World', in *Randall Jarrell: 1914–1965*, eds Robert
      Lowell, Peter Taylor, and Robert Penn Warren (New York:
      Farrar, Straus and Giroux), pp. 48–62. Reprinted in *Modern
      American Poetry*, ed. Guy Owens (Deland, Fla.: Everett
      Edwards, 1972), pp. 205–15.

87   'William Carlos Williams's Poetic Language', in *Twentieth
      Century Views on William Carlos Williams*, ed. J. Hillis Miller
      (Englewood Cliffs, N.J.: Prentice-Hall), pp. 121–31.
      Reprinted as 'Williams, a Redeeming Voice', in *The Ordinary
      Universe* (1968), pp.180–93.

88   'The Human Image in Yeats', *University Review* (Dublin)
      3, no. 8, pp. 56–70. Reprinted in *The Ordinary Universe*
      (1968), pp. 108–24.

89   'Literary Fascism', *Commentary* 44 (11 November), p. 82.

90   'Swift's Perspectives', *Studies* 56 (Autumn), pp. 248–65.

91   'Clashing Symbols', *New York Times Book Review* (10
      December), pp. 12, 14, 16 (Review of *Eminent Domain* by
      Richard Ellmann).

92   'Kenneth Burke's Dangling Novel', *Encounter* 29 (October),
      pp. 78–84 (Review of the reissued *Towards a Better Life* by
      Kenneth Burke).

93   'Magic Defeated', *New York Review of Books* 9, no. 8 (17
      November), pp. 22–5 (Review of *The Time of Angels* by Iris
      Murdoch, *The Birds Fall Down* by Rebecca West, and *The
      Animal Hotel* by Jean Garrigue).

94   'Moidores for Hart Crane', *New York Review of Books* 9,
      no. 8 (9 November), pp. 16–19 (Review of *The Poetry of
      Hart Crane* by W. B. Lewis). Reprinted as 'Hart Crane', in
      Reading America (1987), pp. 242–50

95   'O Mailer, O America', *Listener* 78, no. 2012 (19 October),
      pp. 505–6 (Review of *Cannibals and Christians* by Norman
      Mailer).

96   'The Politics of Poetry', *New York Review of Books* 8, no.
      6 (6 April), pp. 22–5 (Review of *W. B. Yeats and Georgian
      Ireland* by Donald Torchia).

97   'Sweepstakes', *New York Review of Books* 9, no. 6 (28
      September), pp. 5–6 (Review of *Why Are We in Vietnam?*

by Norman Mailer, *Death Kit* by Susan Sontag, and *The Puzzlehead Girl* by Christina Stead).

1968

98   *The Ordinary Universe: Soundings in Modern Literature* (London: Faber and Faber; New York: Macmillan), 320 pp. Reissued in paperback, 1987 (New York: Ecco Press).

99   (Ed.), *Swift Revisited* (Cork: Mercier Press; Hatboro, Penn.: Folklore Associates), 89 pp.

100   'Swift as Poet', in *Swift Revisited*, pp. 75–89.

101   'A View of Mansfield Park', in *Critical Essays on Jane Austen*, ed. B. C. Southam (London: Routledge and Kegan Paul), pp. 39–59. Reprinted in *England, Their England* (1988), pp. 118–28.

102   'University Professor', *Studies* 57 (Autumn), pp. 284–8.

103   Review of *Barbarous Knowledge: Myth in the Poetry of Yeats, Graves and Muir* by Daniel Hoffman, *Modern Language Quarterly* 29, no. 1 (March), pp. 120–1.

104   'Criterion Omnia', *Cambridge Review* 89, no. 2164 (9 February), pp. 257–60 (Review of *The Criterion* [18 vols.], ed. T. S. Eliot).

105   'Scenes of Artistic Life', *Listener* 80, no. 2065 (24 October), pp. 539–40 (Review of *George Eliot* by Gordon Haight).

1969

106   *Jonathan Swift: A Critical Introduction* (London: Cambridge University Press), viii, 235 pp.

107   *Emily Dickinson* (Minneapolis: University of Minnesota Press), 47 pp. Reprinted in *Six American Poets from Emily Dickinson to the Present*, ed. Allen Tate (Minneapolis: University of Minnesota Press, 1972), pp. 9–44.

108   'The Other Emily', in *The Brontës: A Collection of Critical Essays*, ed. Ian Gregor (Englewood Cliffs, N.J.: Prentice-Hall), pp. 157–72.

109   'The Proper Plenitude of Fact', in *Twentieth Century Views on Marianne Moore*, ed. Charles Tomlinson (Englewood

Cliffs, N.J.: Prentice-Hall), pp. 165–71. Reprinted from
The Ordinary Universe (1968), pp. 21–50.

110   'Walt Whitman', in *Walt Whitman: A Critical Anthology*,
ed. Francis Murphy (Harmondsworth: Penguin), pp. 427–49.
Reprinted from *Connoisseurs of Chaos* (1965), pp. 23–51.

111   'On Santayana', *Cambridge Review* 90, no. 2191 (9 May),
pp. 344–7 (Review of *Selected Critical Writings of George
Santayana*, ed. Norman Henfrey).

112   'The Cooling of Admiration: Pound's Interest in a Protégé
of Yeats', *Times Literary Supplement* 3497 (6 March),
pp. 239–40 (Review of *Pound/Joyce: The Letters of Ezra
Pound to James Joyce*, ed. Forrest Read). Reprinted as
'James Joyce', in *We Irish* (1986), pp. 100–6.

113   'Then, Now, and Always', *Southern Review* 5, no. 4,
pp. 1236–49 (Review of recently published books).

114   'A Very Special Case', *New York Review of Books* 12, no.
1 (16 January), pp. 10–12 (Review of *Swift: The Man, His
Works and the Age; Vol. 2, Dr Swift* by Irvin Ehrenpreis).

1970

115   'Donne', in *Atlantic Brief Lives*, ed. Louis Kronenberger
(Boston: Little, Brown), pp. 231–4.

116   'Fielding', in *Atlantic Brief Lives*, ed. Louis Kronenberger
(Boston: Little, Brown), pp. 271–3.

117   'T. S. Eliot's *Four Quartets*: A New Reading', in *T. S.
Eliot's Quartets: A Selection of Critical Essays*, ed. Bernard
Bergonzi (London: Macmillan; Nashville, Tenn.: Aurora
Publishers), pp. 212–38.

118   'The English Dickens and *Dombey and Son*', *Dickens
Centenary Volume, Nineteenth Century Fiction* 24, no. 4
(March), pp. 383–403. Reprinted in *Dickens Centennial
Essays*, eds Ada Nisbit and Blake Nevius, pp. 1–21.

119   'Babel's Icons', *Art International* 14, no. 6 (Summer),
pp. 40–2.

120   'On the Contrary', *Art International* 14, no. 9 (November),
pp. 17–18.

121   'Keeping Faith with a Broken Music: The Criticism of

Walter Benjamin', *Listener* 84, no. 2158 (6 August), pp. 184–5.

122   'Pound's *Mauberley* and a Source in Henry James's *The Awkward Age*', *Notes and Queries* 17, no. 2 (February), pp. 49–50.

123   'Saint Language: The Holy Language of Modernism', *Art International* 14, no. 2 (February), pp. 18–20, 27. Reprinted in *Literary Language since Shakespeare*, ed. George Watson (London and New York: Oxford University Press), pp. 386–407.

124   'Golden Dawn', *Listener* 84, no. 2166 (1 October), p. 457 (Review of *Ah, Sweet Dancer: A Correspondence between W. B. Yeats and Margot Ruddock*, ed. Roger McHugh).

125   'Lowell's Seasons', *Manchester Guardian Weekly* 103 (26 December), p. 58 (Review of *Notebook* by Robert Lowell).

1971

126   (Ed.), *Jonathan Swift: A Critical Anthology*, Penguin Critical Anthologies (Harmondsworth and Baltimore: Penguin), 455 pp.

127   *William Butler Yeats*, Modern Masters Series (London: Fontana; New York: Viking Press), 139 pp. Reissued in paperback, 1988 (New York: Ecco Press), xiii, 160pp.

128   'Emily Brontë: On the Latitude of Interpretation', in *The Interpretation of Narrative*, ed. Morton Bloomfield (Cambridge, Mass.: Harvard University Press), pp. 105–33. Reprinted in *England, Their England* (1988), pp. 149–76.

129   'The English Dickens and *Dombey and Son*', in *Dickens Centennial Essays*, eds Ada Nisbit and Blake Nevius (Berkeley: University of California Press), pp. 1–21. Reprinted from *Nineteenth Century Fiction* 24, no. 4 (1970). Reprinted in *England, Their England* (1988), pp. 177–97.

130   'On Sterne, Our Contemporary', in *The Winged Skull: Papers on Sterne*, eds Arthur H. Cash and John M. Stedmond (London: Methuen; Kent, Ohio: Kent State University Press), pp. 42–58. Reprinted in *England, Their England* (1988), pp. 101–17.

131   'The Eye as Benevolent Despot', *Art International* 15, no. 5 (May), pp. 28–31.

132   'The Mind's Eye', *Art International* 15, no. 7 (September), pp. 22–5.

133   'The Purer Eye', *Art International* 15, no. 6 (June), pp. 22–4.

134   'Life Sentence', *New York Review of Books* 17, no. 9 (2 December), pp. 28–30 (Review of *Meet Me in Green Glen* by Robert Penn Warren, *The Condor Passes* by Shirley Ann Grau, and *Edsel* by Karl Shapiro).

1972

135   (Ed.), *Memoirs: Autobiography – First Draft* by W. B. Yeats (London and New York: Macmillan), 318 pp.

136   'Emily Dickinson', in *Six American Poets*, ed. Allen Tate (Minneapolis: University of Minnesota Press), pp. 9–44. Reprinted from *Emily Dickinson* (1969).

137   Introduction to *Memoirs* by W. B. Yeats, pp. 9–15.

138   'The Lost World of Randall Jarrell', in *Modern American Poetry: Essays in Criticism*, ed. Guy Owens (Deland, Fla.: Everett Edwards), pp. 205–15. Reprinted from *Randall Jarrell: 1914–65* (1967), pp. 48–62.

139   'On Allen Tate', in *Allen Tate and His Work: Critical Evaluations*, ed. Radcliffe Squires (Minneapolis: University of Minnesota Press), pp. 287–90.

140   'Williams: A Redeeming Language', in *William Carlos Williams*, ed. Charles Tomlinson (London: Penguin), pp. 383–8. Reprinted and abridged from *The Ordinary Universe* (1968).

141   'The American *Wasteland* at Fifty', *Art International* 16, no. 5 (20 May), pp. 61–4, 67.

142   'The Conspiratorial Rhetoric of Dr. Leavis', *Spectator* 229 (15 July), pp. 92–3.

143   'God with Thunder: T. S. Eliot Memorial Lectures', *Times Literary Supplement* 3687 (3 November), pp. 1339–40.

144   'The Problem of Being Irish', *Times Literary Supplement* 3655 (17 March), pp. 291–2. Reprinted as 'Another Complex Fate', in *We Irish* (1986), pp. 141–7.

145 'Prometheus in Straits: T. S. Eliot Memorial Lectures', *Times Literary Supplement* 3688 (10 November), pp. 1371–3.
146 'View from Dublin', *Atlantic* 229 (May), pp. 12, 14–17.
147 'The Quatercentenary of John Donne', *Spectator* 229 (18 November), pp. 795–6.
148 (With Frank Kermode), 'Yeats, Jongsen, Jannsen: an Error in the Text of Yeats's *Autobiography*', *Times Literary Supplement* 3650 (11 February), p. 157.
149 Review of *Eliot and His Age* by Russell Kirk and *T. S. Eliot's Intellectual Development* by John Margolis, *Commonweal* 96, no. 10 (12 May), pp. 242–4.
150 Review of *The World of Charles Dickens* by Angus Wilson, *Nineteenth Century* 22, no. 2 (September), pp. 216–18.

1973

151 *W. B. Yeats*, tr. Claude Guillot (Paris: Editions Seghers), 163 pp.
152 'Emily Brontë: On the Latitude of Interpretation', in *Emily Brontë: Penguin Critical Anthology*, ed. Jean-Pierre Petit (Harmondsworth: Penguin), pp. 296–324. Reprinted from *The Interpretation of Narrative* (1971), pp. 105–33.
153 'Till the Fight is Finished: Lawrence and his Letters', in *D. H. Lawrence: Novelist, Poet, Prophet*, ed. Stephen Spender (London: Weidenfeld and Nicholson), pp. 197–209. Reprinted as 'D. H. Lawrence and his Letters', in *England, Their England* (1988), pp. 275–89.
154 'Walt Whitman's Poetry', in *American Literature to 1900*, ed. Marcus Cunliffe (London: Sphere Books), pp. 258–86. Reprinted in *The New History of Literature: American Literature to 1900*, ed. Marcus Cunliffe (New York: Bedrick, 1987), pp. 227–51. Also reprinted in *Reading America* (1987), pp. 68–96.
155 'Yeats and the Living Voice', in *Issues in Contemporary Literary Criticism*, ed. Gregory T. Polletta (Boston: Little, Brown), pp. 445–61.
156 'La Parola nella Parola', tr. Giovanna Morisiani, *Paragone* 280 (June), pp. 5–24.

157 'Le problème d'être irlandais', tr. Viviane Forrester, *Les Lettres Nouvelles* (March), pp. 105–15. Translated from *Times Literary Supplement* 3655 (17 March 1972).

158 'Thieves of Fire: Melville and Dostoevsky', *Atlantis* 5 (April), pp. 108–22. Text of T. S. Eliot Memorial Lecture of November 1972.

159 'Viewpoint', *Times Literary Supplement* 3702 (16 February), p. 178.

160 'Accidents and Accusations', *New Statesman* 86 (31 August), pp. 286–7 (Review of *History; For Lizzie and Harriet* and *The Dolphin* by Robert Lowell).

161 'Good God', *New York Review of Books* 20, no. 12 (19 July), pp. 17–18 (Review of *Epistle to a Godson and Other Poems* and *Forewords and Afterwords* by W. H. Auden). Reprinted as 'Auden's *Epistle to a Godson*', in *W. H. Auden: The Critical Heritage*, ed. John Haffenden (London: Routledge and Kegan Paul, 1983), pp. 480–4. Also reprinted as 'Auden II', in *Reading America* (1987), pp. 258–64.

162 'Towards a Hermeneutics of Shakespearian Tragedy', *Commonweal* 98, no. 1 (9 March), pp. 17–18 (Review of *Shakespeare's God: The Role of Religion in the Tragedies* by Ivor Morris).

163 'A Visit to Greenland', *Commonweal* 99, no. 9 (30 November), pp. 241–2 (Review of *The Honorary Consul* by Graham Greene).

1974

164 *Imagination* (Glasgow: University of Glasgow Press), 40 pp. (Adapted from 1974 W. P. Ker Memorial Lectures at the University of Glasgow). Reprinted as Chapter 2 of *The Sovereign Ghost* (1977).

165 *Thieves of Fire* (London: Faber and Faber; New York: Oxford University Press), 139 pp.

166 'Saul Bellow and the *Dangling Man*', in *Saul Bellow: A Collection of Critical Essays*, ed. Earl Rovit (Englewood Cliffs, N.J.: Prentice-Hall), pp. 19–30.

167 'The Word within a Word', in *The Waste Land in Different*

Voices, ed. A. D. Moody (London: Edward Arnold; New York: St Martin's Press), pp. 185–201. Revised and reprinted in *The Sovereign Ghost* (1977), pp. 183–206.

168 'Allen Tate's Seventy-Fifth Birthday', *Times Literary Supplement* 3797 (13 December), p. 1414.

169 'The American Style of Failure', *Sewanee Review* 82, no. 3 (Summer), pp. 407–32. Expanded and reprinted in *The Sovereign Ghost* (1977), pp. 103–27.

170 'Ezra Pound: Periplum', *Paideuma* 3, no. 2 (Autumn), pp. 151–68.

171 'The Politics of Yeats's Theatre', *Threshold* 25 (June), pp. 27–33.

172 'A Reply to Frank Kermode', *Critical Inquiry* 1, no. 2 (December), pp. 447–52. Reprinted as 'The Good Soldier', in *England, Their England* (1988), pp. 256–74.

173 'Between Fact and Value', *Times Literary Supplement* 3796 (6 December), p. 1358 (Review of *The Rhetoric of Irony* by Wayne C. Booth).

174 'Fire in the Great Vein', *New Review* 1, no. 5 (August), pp. 69–72 (Review of *Collected Poems* by Austin Clarke).

175 Review of *The Harvard Concordance of Shakespeare* by Marvin Spevack and *The Riverside Shakespeare*, ed. G. Blackmore Evans, *New York Times Book Review* (7 April), p. 23.

176 'Some Versions of Empson', *Times Literary Supplement* 3770 (7 June), pp. 597–8 (Review of *William Empson: The Man and His Work* by Roma Gill).

177 'The Will to Certitude', *Times Literary Supplement* 3782 (30 August), pp. 917–18 (Review of *Uncollected Essays and Reviews* by Yvor Winters and *The Complex of Yvor Winters* by Richard J. Sexton).

1975

178 (Ed.), *Seven American Poets from MacLeish to Nemerov* (Minneapolis: University of Minnesota Press), 329 pp.

179 'Eliot's *Four Quartets*', in *Twentieth Century Poetry: Critical Essays and Documents*, eds Graham Martin and P. N. Furbank (London: The Open University Press),

pp. 303–24. Reprinted from *T. S. Eliot's Quartets*, ed. Bernard Bergonzi (1970), pp. 212–380.

180   'Mediacy and Immediacy: A Note on Geoffrey Hartman', *Times Literary Supplement* 3832 (22 August), pp. 934–5.

181   'Thoughts after Salzburg', *Times Literary Supplement* 3823 (13 June), p. 658.

182   'A. R. Ammons and the Lesser Celandine', *Parnassus* 3, no. 2, pp. 19–26 (Review of *Sphere: The Form of a Motion* by A. R. Ammons).

183   'An Ear for Fiction', *Times Literary Supplement* 3804 (31 January), p. 103 (Review of *E. M. Forster: Aspects of the Novel*, ed. Oliver Stallybrass).

184   'A Fantastic Heart', *New Republic* 172, no. 17 (26 April), pp. 19–21 (Review of *The Letters of Sean O'Casey, Volume 1 (1910–1941)*, ed. David Krause). Reprinted as 'Sean O'Casey', in *We Irish* (1986), pp. 226–9.

185   'The Habits of the Poet', *Times Literary Supplement* 3816 (25 April), pp. 442–3 (Review of *Poetry of Change* and *To All Appearances* by Josephine Miles).

186   'Irish Tragedy', *Spectator* 7651 (15 February), pp. 182–3 (Review of *Ireland: The War Years* by Joseph Carroll and *Hell or Connaught* by Peter B. Ellis). Reprinted as 'De Valera's Day', in *We Irish* (1986), pp. 161–4.

187   'Mr. Pleasure', *New Republic* 172, no. 11 (15 March), pp. 25–8 (Review of *The Evening Colonnade* by Cyril Connolly).

188   'Reconsiderations', *New Republic* 173, no. 16 (18 October), pp. 29–31 (Review of the reissued *Towards a Better Life* by Kenneth Burke).

1976

189   *The Sovereign Ghost: Studies in Imagination* (Los Angeles and Berkeley: University of California Press), 229 pp. English edn (London: Faber and Faber, 1978). Reissued in paperback, 1990 (New York: Ecco Press).

190   'The Concept of Romantic Ireland', in *Yeats, Sligo and Ireland*, ed. A. N. Jeffares (Totowa, N.J.: Barnes and

Noble; Gerrards Cross: Colin Smythe, 1980), pp. 17–30. Reprinted in *We Irish* (1986), pp. 21–33.

191   'John Butler Yeats in America', in *Abroad in America 1776–1914*, eds Marc Pachter and Francis Wein (Washington, D.C.: Smithsonian Institute), pp. 260–9.

192   'Being Irish Together', *Sewanee Review* 84, no. 1 (Winter), pp. 129–33. Reprinted as 'Together', in *We Irish* (1986), pp. 148–52.

193   'Imagination: The Sovereign Ghost', *Sewanee Review* 84, no. 1 (Winter), pp. 98–118.

194   'Imagination: The Sovereign Ghost II', *Sewanee Review* 84, no. 2 (Spring), pp. 248–74.

195   'Nuances of a Theme by Allen Tate', *Southern Review* 12, no. 4 (Autumn), pp. 698–714.

196   'On Gulliver's Travels: The Brainwashing of Lemuel Gulliver', *Listener* 96, no. 2482 (4 November), pp. 578–9.

197   Review of *The Art of Ted Hughes* by Keith Sagar, *New Republic* 173, no. 5 (31 January), pp. 30–1.

198   'Drums under the Window', *New York Review of Books* 23, no. 16 (14 October), pp. 12–15 (Review of *The Damnable Question* by George Dangerfield and *Mother Ireland* by Edna O'Brien). Reprinted in *We Irish* (1986), pp. 153–60.

199   'Emily Dickinson: The Poetry of Excruciation', *Times Literary Supplement* 3869 (7 May), pp. 538–9 (Review of recently published books of and on Emily Dickinson's poetry). Reprinted in *Reading America* (1987), pp. 97–110.

200   'Lives of the Poets', *Partisan Review* 43, no. 1, pp. 135–8 (Review of *Three on a Tower: The Lives and Works of Ezra Pound, T. S. Eliot and William Carlos Williams* by Louis Simpson).

201   'The Master Mystic', *Times Literary Supplement* 3863 (26 March), p. 334 (Review of *That Myriad-Minded Man: A Biography of G. W. Russell-AE* by Henry Summerfield). Reprinted as 'AE', in *We Irish* (1986), pp. 197–203.

202   'Mirrors of Conflict', *New York Times Book Review* (2 May), pp. 2–3 (Review of *Keywords* by Raymond Williams). Reprinted as 'Raymond Williams', in *England, Their England* (1988), pp. 351–8.

203   Review of *Representations: Essays on Literature and Society* by Steven Marcus, *New York Times Book Review* (21 March), pp. 7–8.

204   'Southern Style', *Times Literary Supplement* 3876 (25 June), p. 756 (Review of *The Possibilities of Order: Cleanth Brooks and His Works*, ed. Lewis P. Simpson).

205   Review of *The Story-Shaped World: Fiction and Metaphysics* by Brian Wicker, *Commonweal* 103, no. 11 (21 May), pp. 347–8.

1977

206   'Eliot and *The Criterion*', in *The Literary Criticism of T. S. Eliot*, ed. David Newton-De Molina (London: Athlone Press, University of London), pp. 20–41.

207   'Yeats: The Question of Symbolism', in *Myth and Reality in Irish Literature*, ed. Joseph Ronsley (Waterloo, Ont.: Wilfrid Laurier University Press), pp. 99–115. Reprinted in *The Symbolist Movement in the Literature of European Languages*, ed. Anna Balakian (Budapest: Akademiai Kiado, 1982), pp. 279–93. Also reprinted in *We Irish* (1986), pp. 34–51.

208   'On the Limits of a Language', *Sewanee Review* 85 (Summer), pp. 371–91. Reprinted in *The Arts without Mystery* (1983), pp. 131–43.

209   'Beyond Truth to Troth', *Times Literary Supplement* 3926 (10 June), pp. 705–6 (Review of *Complementarities: Uncollected Essays* by I. A. Richards).

210   'Mediterranean Man', *Partisan Review* 44, pp. 452–7 (Review of *Ezra Pound* by Donald Davie).

211   'Moving and Desperate', *New York Times Book Review* (11 December), pp. 13, 45 (Review of *Collected Poems 1919–76* by Allen Tate). Reprinted as 'Allen Tate', in *Reading America* (1987), pp. 230–6.

212   Review of *Of Grammatology* by Jacques Derrida, *New Republic* 176, no. 16 (16 April), pp. 32–4.

213   'The Passing Day', *Spectator* 7748 (1 January), pp. 33–5 (Review of *Hail and Farewell: Ave, Salve, Vale* by George

Moore, ed. Richard Cave). Reprinted as 'George Moore', in *We Irish* (1986), pp. 214–17.

214   'Readers and Rap Sessions', *Times Literary Supplement* 3918 (15 April), p. 447 (Review of *Hamlet's Castle: The Study of Literature as a Social Experience* by Gordon Mills).

215   'A Vocation for Remorse', *Times Literary Supplement* 3939 (9 September), p. 1087 (Review of *Reothairtis is Contraigh, Spring Tide and Neap Tide* by Sorley Maclean).

1978

216   (Ed. and Introduction), *Poems of R. P. Blackmur* (Princeton: Princeton University Press), 53 pp.

217   'Coming Together in Ireland?', *Listener* 100, no. 2586 (16 November), pp. 2–3. Transcription of 'Personal View', on BBC Radio 3.

218   'Does America have a Major Poet?', *New York Times Book Review* (3 December), pp. 9, 88.

219   'Lionel Trilling, Mind and Society', *Sewanee Review* 86, no. 2 (Spring), pp. 161–86. Reprinted in *Reading America* (1987), pp. 175–98.

220   'The Literature of Trouble', *Hibernia* (11 May), (abridged from lecture given at Princeton University). Full text reprinted in *We Irish* (1986), pp. 182–94.

221   'Bair's Beckett', *Magill* (September). Reprinted in *We Irish* (1986), pp. 253–7.

222   'Five Hundred Years of the King's English', *New York Review of Books* 25 (1 June), pp. 30–2 (Review of various recent publications about the Oxford University Press). Reprinted as 'The Story of English III', in *England, Their England* (1988), pp. 19–25.

223   'Lowell at the End', *Hudson Review* 31 (Spring), pp. 196–201 (Review of *Day by Day* by Robert Lowell). Reprinted in *Reading America* (1987), pp. 281–6.

224   'Poets and their Predicates', *Times Literary Supplement* 3981 (27 July), pp. 810–11 (Review of *Five Temperaments* by David Calstone).

225   'So Long as it was Verbal', *New Review* 5, no. 2 (Autumn), pp. 94–8 (Review of *The Selected Letters of Conrad Aiken*,

ed. Joseph Killorin). Reprinted as 'Conrad Aiken', in *Reading America* (1987), pp. 199–205.

226 'Themes from Derek Walcott', *Parnassus* 6, no. 1, pp. 88–100 (Review of *Sea Grapes* by Derek Walcott).

227 'Wiring up the New Place', *Times Literary Supplement* 3970 (5 May), p. 499 (Review of *A Homemade World* by Hugh Kenner).

1979

228 (With Robert W. Burchfield and Andrew Timothy), *The Quality of Spoken English on BBC Radio: A Report for the BBC* (London: British Broadcasting Corporation), 24 pp.

229 'One Way Communication', *Sewanee Review* 87, no. 3 (Summer), pp. 383–435. Reprinted in *Image and Illusion: Anglo-Irish Literature and its Contexts, A Festschrift for Roger McHugh*, ed. Maurice Harmon (Dublin: Wolfhound Press, 1979), pp. 119–41.

230 'The Authority of Ruins', *New Statesman* 97, no. 2507 (6 April), pp. 485–6 (Review of *Samuel Beckett: The Critical Heritage*, eds Lawrence Grover and Raymond Federman).

231 'England Englished', *New York Times Book Review* (29 April), pp. 3, 56 (Review of *The Reader Over Your Shoulder* by Robert Graves and Alan Hodge). Reprinted as 'The Story of English IV', in *England, Their England* (1988), pp. 25–30.

232 'From the Country of the Blue', *New York Review of Books* 26, no. 2 (22 February), pp. 37–9 (Review of *The Poems of George Meredith*, ed. Phyllis B. Bartley). Reprinted as 'Meredith's Poems', in *England, Their England* (1988), pp. 243–55.

233 'Hannah Arendt and *The Life of the Mind*', *Hudson Review* 32, no. 2 (Summer), pp. 281–8 (Review of *The Life of the Mind: Thinking; Willing* by Hannah Arendt).

234 'The Heart in Hiding', *New York Review of Books* 26, no. 14 (27 September), pp. 51–3 (Review of *Gerard Manley Hopkins: A Biography* by Paddy Kitchen). Reprinted as 'Hopkins', in *England, Their England* (1988), pp. 218–27.

235 'Literary Despots', *New York Times Book Review*

(4 February), pp. 12, 28–30 (Review of *Hart Crane and Yvor Winters: Their Literary Correspondence* by Thomas Parkinson). Reprinted in *Reading America* (1987), pp. 250–3.

236   'The Stains of Ireland', *New York Review of Books* 26, no. 10 (14 June), pp. 21–3 (Review of *The Year of the French* by Thomas Flanagan). Reprinted as 'The Year of the French', in *We Irish* (1986), pp. 21–3.

1980

237   Foreword to *Henry Adams* by R. P. Blackmur, ed. Veronica A. Makowsky (New York: Harcourt Brace Jovanovich), pp. vii–xiii.

238   Preface to *The Informer* by Liam O'Flaherty (New York: Harcourt Brace Jovanovich), pp. iii–xii.

239   'The American Imagination', in *America and Ireland 1776–1976: The American Identity and the Irish Connection*, eds Owen Dudley Edwards and David Noel Doyle (Westport, Conn.: Greenwood Press), pp. 69–78.

240   'Radio Talk', in *The State of the Language*, eds Leonard Michaels and Christopher Ricks (Berkeley and Los Angeles: University of California Press), pp. 539–52. Reprinted and abridged as 'Dialogue of One', in *Ferocious Alphabets* (1981), pp. 3–18.

241   'Romantic Ireland', in *Yeats, Sligo, and Ireland* (1976), pp. 17–30. Reprinted in *We Irish* (1986), pp. 21–33.

242   'The Definition of Humanism', Script for one-hour programme on National Public Radio series *A Question of Place: Sound Portraits of Twentieth Century Humanists*.

243   'Listening to the Saddest Story', *Sewanee Review* 88, no. 4 (Fall), pp. 557–71. Reprinted in *The Presence of Ford Madox Ford*, ed. Sondra J. Stang (Philadelphia: University of Pennsylvania Press, 1981), pp. 44–54. Also reprinted as 'The Good Soldier', In *England, Their England* (1988), pp. 256–74.

244   'Shakespeare at Sonnets', *Sewanee Review* 88, no. 3 (Summer), pp. 463–73.

245 'State of Criticism: French Structuralist Theories', *Partisan Review* 47, no. 3, pp. 397–409.

246 'Two Notes on Stevens', *Wallace Stevens Journal* 4, pp. 40–5.

247 'Anxious Lives', *New York Times Book Review* (6 April), pp. 11, 19 (Review of *Autobiography: Essays Theoretical and Critical*, ed. James Olney).

248 Review of *Blue Wine and Other Poems* by John Hollander, *New York Arts Journal* (November).

249 'A Culture to Escape Into', *New York Times Book Review* (28 September), pp. 11, 32 (Review of *The Victorians and Ancient Greece* by Richard Jenkyns).

250 'Deconstructing Deconstruction', *New York Review of Books* 27, no. 10 (12 June), pp. 37–41 (Review of *Deconstruction and Criticism* by Harold Bloom, Paul de Man, Jacques Derrida, Geoffrey H. Hartman, and J. Hillis Miller and *Allegories of Reading* by Paul de Man).

251 'New York Poets', *New York Review of Books* 27, no. 13 (14 August), pp. 49–50 (Review of books by Kenneth Koch, James Schuyler, Frederick Seidel, and Robert Mazzocco).

252 'Of Self and Society', *New York Times Book Review* (20 January), p. 9 (Review of *Prefaces to the Experience of Literature* by Lionel Trilling and *The Last Decade: Essays and Reviews 1965–1975* by Lionel Trilling, ed. Diana Trilling).

253 'The Onward March of Obsolescence', *Times Literary Supplement* 4033 (11 July), p. 775 (Review of *The Republic of Letters: A History of Postwar American Literary Opinion* by Grant Webster).

254 'Poets of Plenty', *New York Times Book Review* (23 March), pp. 11, 32 (Review of *Part of Nature, Part of Us: Modern American Poets* by Helen Vendler).

255 'Reading about Writing', *New York Times Book Review* (9 November), pp. 11, 32–3 (Review of *Criticism in the Wilderness: The Study of Literature Today* by Geoffrey H. Hartman).

256 'Sign Language', *New York Review of Books* 26, nos 21–2 (24 January), pp. 36–9 (Review of *As We Know* by John

Ashbery). Reprinted as 'John Ashbery I', in *Reading America* (1987), pp. 302–11.

257 Review of *Structuralism and Since: From Lévi-Strauss to Derrida*, ed. John Sturrock, *New Republic* 182, no. 21 (24 May), pp. 32–4.

258 'What the Ouija Board Said', *New York Times Book Review* (15 June), pp. 11, 20 (Review of *Scripts for the Pageant* by James Merrill).

259 'You Better Believe It', *New York Review of Books* 27, no. 18 (20 November), pp. 20–2 (Review of *The Middle Ground* by Margaret Drabble and *Setting the World on Fire* by Angus Wilson).

1981

260 *Ferocious Alphabets* (London: Faber and Faber; Boston: Little, Brown), xiv, 211 pp. Reissued in paperback, 1984 (New York: Columbia University Press).

261 'Listening to the Saddest Story', in *The Presence of Ford Madox Ford*, ed. Sondra J. Stang (Philadelphia: University of Pennsylvania Press), pp. 44–54. Reprinted from *Sewanee Review* 88, no. 4 (Fall 1980), pp. 557–71. Reprinted as 'The Good Soldier', in *England, Their England* (1988), pp. 256–74.

262 'The Hunger Strikers', *New York Review of Books* 28, no. 16, (22 October), pp. 29–31.

263 'Inside the Maze–legitimising heirs to the men of 1916', *Listener* 106, no. 2725 (3 September), pp. 226–8. Text of Radio 3 broadcast.

264 'Leavis and Eliot', *Raritan Review* 1, no. 1 (Summer), pp. 68–87. Reprinted as 'Leavis on Eliot', in *England, Their England* (1988), pp. 332–50.

265 'Modern Literary Theory: Its Place in Teaching', *Times Literary Supplement* 4062 (6 February), pp. 135–6. Contribution to symposium.

266 'S/S/S: Signs, Systems, Structures: A Documentary Essay on Structuralism and Post-Structuralism', BBC Radio 3 (6 September, repeat 9 December).

267 'A Snitch who became the Intellectuals' Darling', *Listener* 106, no. 2741 (31 December), pp. 813–14. Text from Radio 3 broadcast.

268 'Castle Catholic', *Times Literary Supplement* 4087 (31 July), p. 871 (Review of *Voices and the Sound of Drums: An Irish Autobiography* by Patrick Shea). Reprinted in *We Irish* (1986), pp. 165–8.

269 'The General Critic's Business', *Times Literary Supplement* 4091 (28 August), pp. 971–2 (Review of *Matthew Arnold: A Life* by Park Honan). Reprinted as 'Arnold as Critic', in *England, Their England* (1988), pp. 198–207.

270 Review of *I, Vincent! (Poems from the Paintings of Van Gogh)* by Robert Fagles, *Southern Review* 17, no. 3 (Summer), pp. 611–13.

271 'I've Another Little Story For You', *New York Times Book Review* (20 September), pp. 3, 28 (Review of *Collected Stories* by Frank O'Connor). Reprinted as 'Frank O'Connor', in *We Irish* (1986), pp. 230–4.

272 'Making Room for the Reader', *Times Literary Supplement* 4075 (8 May), pp. 507–8 (Review of *Is There a Text in This Class?: The Authority of Interpretive Communities* by Stanley Fish).

273 'More Poetry than Prose', *New York Times Book Review* (6 September), pp. 6, 17 (Review of *Shadow Train* by John Ashbery). Reprinted as 'John Ashbery II', in *Reading America* (1987), pp. 312–15.

274 'The Poet Young', *New York Times Book Review* (9 August), pp. 8–9, 27 (Review of *Early Auden* by Edward Mendelson). Reprinted as 'Auden I', in *Reading America* (1987), pp. 254–8.

275 'In Praise of Gone Times', *Times Literary Supplement* 4086 (24 July), p. 832 (Review of *The Parochialism of the Present: Contemporary Issues in Education* by G. H. Bantock).

276 'The Real McCoy', *New York Review of Books* 28, no. 18 (19 November), pp. 44–7 (Review of *Essays on Realism* by Georg Lukács, ed. Rodney Livingstone, tr. David Fernbach and *The Realistic Imagination: English Fiction from Frankenstein to Lady Chatterley* by George Levine).

277 'Secret Sharer', *New York Review of Books* 28, no. 2 (19

February), pp. 15–17 (Review of *Ways of Escape* by Graham Greene). Reprinted as 'Graham Greene, Autobiographer', in *England, Their England* (1988), pp. 323–31.

278   'Should Novels Argue?', *New York Times Book Review* (18 January), pp. 9, 27 (Review of *Ideas and the Novel* by Mary McCarthy).

279   Review of *Threshold of a Nation: A Study in English and Irish Drama* by Philip Edwards, *Renaissance Quarterly* 34, no. 2 (Summer), pp. 279–82.

280   'Walter Pater's Renaissance', *New York Review of Books* 28, no. 8 (14 May), pp. 40–3 (Review of *The Renaissance Studies in Art and Poetry [The 1893 text]*, ed. Donald L. Hill and *Walter Pater's Art of Autobiography* by Gerald Monsman). Reprinted as 'Pater's *Renaissance*', in *England, Their England* (1988), pp. 208–17.

281   'You Could Say She Had a Calling for Death', *New York Times Book Review* (22 November), pp. 1, 30–1 (Review of *Collected Poems* by Sylvia Plath). Reprinted as 'Sylvia Plath', in *Reading America* (1987), pp. 296–301.

1982

282   'Eliot in Fair Colonus: "The Elder Statesman"', in *T. S. Eliot: The Critical Heritage*, Vol. 2, ed. Michael Grant (London: Routledge and Kegan Paul), pp. 712–22. Reprinted from *Studies* 48 (Spring 1959), pp. 49–58.

283   'The Values of *Moll Flanders*', in *Daniel Defoe: Schriften zum Erzählwerk*, eds R. and H. Heidenreich (Darmstadt: Wissenschaftliche Buchgesellschaft), pp. 126–41. Reprinted from *Sewanee Review* 71, no. 2 (Spring 1963), pp. 287–303. Reprinted in *England, Their England* (1988), pp. 64–78.

284   'Yeats: The Question of Symbolism', in *The Symbolist Movement in the Literature of European Languages*, ed. Anna Balakian (Budapest: Akademiai Kiado), pp. 279–93. Reprinted from *Myth and Reality in Irish Literature* (1977), pp. 99–115. Reprinted in *We Irish* (1986), pp. 34–51.

285   'The Zealots of Explanation', BBC Reith Lecture No. 1,

Listener 108, no. 2786 (11 November), pp. 13–15. Text of BBC Radio 4 broadcast (10 November, repeated on Radio 3, 14 November). Revised and reprinted as 'Of Art and Mystery', *Boston Review* (October 1983), pp. 7–10. Also reprinted in *The Arts Without Mystery* (1983), pp. 11–21.

286 'The Domestication of Outrage', BBC Reith Lecture No. 2, *Listener* 108, no. 2787 (18 November), pp. 15–17. Text of BBC Radio 4 broadcast (17 November, repeated on Radio 3, 21 November). Reprinted in *The Arts Without Mystery* (1983), pp. 31–41. Also reprinted in *The Symbolic Order*, ed. Peter Abbo (London: Falmer Press, 1989), pp. 104–11.

287 'The Parade of Ideas', BBC Reith Lecture No. 3, *Listener* 108, no. 2788 (25 November), pp. 10–12. Text of BBC Radio 4 broadcast (24 November, repeated on Radio 3, 28 November). Reprinted in *The Arts Without Mystery* (1983), pp. 49–59.

288 'The Cherishing Bureaucracy', BBC Reith Lecture No. 4, *Listener* 108, no. 2789 (2 December), pp. 10–13. Text of BBC Radio 4 broadcast (1 December, repeated on Radio 3, 5 December). Reprinted in *The Arts Without Mystery* (1983), pp. 71–81.

289 'The Anxious Object', BBC Reith Lecture No. 5, *Listener* 108, no. 2790 (9 December), pp. 11–14. Text of BBC Radio 4 broadcast (8 December, repeated on Radio 3, 12 December). Reprinted in *The Arts Without Mystery* (1983), pp. 97–106.

290 'A Talent for Conviction', BBC Reith Lecture No. 6, *Listener* 108, no. 2791 (16 December), pp. 11–14. Text of BBC Radio 4 broadcast (15 December, repeated on Radio 3, 19 December). Reprinted in *The Arts Without Mystery* (1983), pp. 119–29.

291 'The Politics of Modern Criticism', *Bennington Review* 13 (June), pp. 2–9. Reprinted as *The Politics of Modern Criticism* (Bennington, Vt.: Bennington College, Chapbooks in Literature Series).

292 'Vladimir Nabokov: The Great Enchanter', *Listener* 107, no. 2752 (18 March), p. 16. Text of Radio 3 broadcast (17 March).

293 'You Learned to Distinguish a Catholic from a Protestant at 100 Yards', *Listener* 108, no. 2785 (4 November), pp. 5–6. Text of BBC Radio 4 interview.

294 'Creation from Catastrophe', *Times Literary Supplement* 4139 (30 July), pp. 811–12 (Review of *Agon: Towards a Theory of Revisionism* and *The Breaking of the Vessels* by Harold Bloom).

295 'A Critic and her Discontents', *Times Literary Supplement* 4116 (19 February), pp. 177–8 (Review of *In Defence of the Imagination: The Charles Eliot Norton Lectures 1979–1980* by Helen Gardner).

296 'Her Deepest Passion was D. H. Lawrence', *New York Times Book Review* (14 February), pp. 3, 26 (Review of *H. D.: The Life and Work of an American Poet* by Janice S. Robinson). Reprinted as 'H. D.', in *Reading America* (1987), pp. 237–41.

297 'Poetries and their Audiences', *New York Times Book Review* (24 January), pp. 10, 20 (Review of *The Place of Poetry: Two Centuries of an Art in Crisis* by Christopher Clausen).

298 'Romantic Ireland', *London Review of Books* 4, no. 2 (4–17 February), pp. 18–19 (Review of *The Collected Stories of Sean O'Faolain*). Reprinted as 'Sean O'Faolain', in *We Irish* (1986), pp. 235–41.

299 'In Search of the Sublime', *Times Literary Supplement* 4151 (22 October), pp. 1147–8 (Review of *A Mingled Yarn: The Life of R. P. Blackmur* by Russell Fraser).

300 Review of *The Second American Revolution and Other Essays (1976–82)* by Gore Vidal, *New York Times Book Review* (2 May), pp. 7, 35.

301 'Suicide was in the Script', *New York Times Book Review* (24 October), pp. 9, 32 (Review of *The Life of John Berryman* by John Haffenden). Reprinted as 'John Berryman', in *Reading America* (1987), pp. 276–80.

302 'The Two Sides of Derek Walcott', *New York Times Book Review* (3 January), p. 5 (Review of *The Fortunate Traveller* by Derek Walcott).

303 'A University for Protestants', *London Review of Books* 4, no. 14 (5–18 August), pp. 11–12 (Review of *A History of Trinity College, Dublin* by R. B. McDowell and D. A. Webb). Reprinted as 'T. C. D.', in *We Irish* (1986), pp. 169–75.

304 'Wolves, Hawks, Bulls, Pigs', *New York Times Book Review* (14 March), pp. 12, 25 (Review of *New Selected Poems* by Ted Hughes).

305 'Wonder Woman', *New York Review of Books* 29, no. 16 (21 October), pp. 12–17 (Review of *A Bloodsmoor Romance* by Joyce Carol Oates).

306 'Wyndham Lewis's Art', *New York Review of Books* 29, no. 7 (29 April), pp. 28–30 (Review of *The Enemy: A Biography of Wyndham Lewis* by Jeffrey Meyers and *Fables of Aggression: Wyndham Lewis, the Modernist as Fascist* by Fredric Jameson). Reprinted as 'Wyndham Lewis', in *England, Their England* (1988), pp. 290–8.

1983

307 *The Arts Without Mystery* (London: BBC Publications; Boston and New York: Little, Brown), 151 pp.

308 'Auden's *Epistle to a Godson*', in *W. H. Auden: The Critical Heritage*, ed. John Haffenden (London: Routledge and Kegan Paul), pp. 480–4. Reprinted from 'Good God', *New York Review of Books* 20, no. 12 (19 July 1973), pp. 17–18 (Review of *Epistle to a Godson and Other Poems* and *Forewords and Afterwords* by W. H. Auden). Reprinted as 'Auden II', in *Reading America* (1987), pp. 258–64.

309 'Of Art and Mystery', *Boston Review* (October), pp. 7–10. Revised and reprinted from 'The Zealots of Explanation', BBC Reith Lecture No. 1 (1982), *Listener* 108, no. 2786 (11 November 1982), pp. 13–15. Also reprinted as Chapter 1 in *The Arts Without Mystery*, pp. 11–29.

310 'R. P. Blackmur and *The Double Agent*', *Sewanee Review* 91, no. 4 (Fall), pp. 634–43.

311 'Big Effects and Hard-worked Perceptions', *New York Times Book Review* (12 June), pp. 7, 40 (Review of *Bartleby in Manhattan and Other Essays* by Elizabeth Hardwick).

312 Review of *Deconstruction, Theory and Practice* by Christopher Norris, *Philosophy and Literature* 7, no. 2 (October), pp. 248–52.

313 'Far-flung Jottings', *Times Literary Supplement* 4192 (5 August), p. 827 (Review of *The Forties: From Notebooks*

130   Bibliography

and Diaries of the Period by Edmund Wilson, ed. Leon Edel).

314   'Ireland and its Discontents', *New York Times Book Review* (30 October), pp. 11, 27 (Review of *The Collected Stories of Sean O'Faolain* by Sean O'Faolain).

315   'Ireland at Swim', *London Review of Books* 5, no. 7 (21 April–4 May), pp. 3–4 (Review of *The Crane Bag Book of Irish Studies 1977–1981*, eds M. P. Hederman and R. Kearney and *A Colder Eye: The Modern Irish Writers* by Hugh Kenner). Reprinted as 'At Swim', in *We Irish* (1986), pp. 176–81.

316   Review of *Literary Theory: An Introduction* by Terry Eagleton, *New York Review of Books* 30, no. 19 (8 December), pp. 43–5.

317   'Materializing the Spiritual', *Times Literary Supplement* 4162 (7 January), p. 6 (Review of *Writing and the Body: The Northcliffe Lectures, 1981* by Gabriel Josipovici).

318   'Rembrandt and Synge and Molly', *London Review of Books* 5, nos 22–3 (1–21 December), p. 15 (Review of *The Collected Letters of John Millington Synge, Volume I: 1871–1907*, ed. Ann Saddlemyer). Reprinted as 'Synge in his Letters', in *We Irish* (1986), pp. 209–13.

319   'A "Southern Californian" Anglo-Irishman', *New York Times Book Review* (5 June), pp. 7, 28–9 (Review of *Yeats* by Douglas Archibald and *Yeats and American Poetry: The Tradition of the Self* by Terence Diggory).

320   'Transforming the World into Feeling', *New York Times Book Review* (30 January), pp. 9, 26 (Review of *The Selected Poetry of Rainer Maria Rilke*, ed. Stephen Mitchell).

321   Review of *The World, The Text, and The Critic* by Edward W. Said, *New Republic* 188, no. 15 (18 April), pp. 30–3.

322   'The Zeal of a Man of Letters', *New York Times Book Review* (18 September), pp. 1, 30–1 (Review of *Hugging the Shore: Essays and Criticism* by John Updike).

1984

323 *Connoisseurs of Chaos: Ideas of Order in Modern American Poetry* (New York: Columbia University Press, Morningside Edition), 293 pp. Revised and expanded from 1965 edition.

324 'Henry Adams's Novels', *Nineteenth Century Fiction* 39, no. 2 (September), pp. 186–201. Reprinted in *Reading America* (1987), pp. 111–26.

325 'The Question of Voice', *Antaeus* 53 (Autumn), pp. 7–25.

326 'Anger and Dismay', *London Review of Books* 6, no. 13 (19 July), pp. 16–17 (Review of *Literary Education: A Revaluation* by James Gribble, *Reconstructing Literature*, ed. Laurence Lerner, and *Counter-Modernism in Current Critical Theory* by Geoffrey Thurley).

327 'Clergyman and Clown', *Times Literary Supplement* 4219 (10 February), pp. 143–4 (Review of *Swift: The Man, His Works, and The Age, Volume Three: Dean Swift* by Irvin Ehrenpreis).

328 'Creative Contrarieties', *Times Literary Supplement* 4227 (6 April), p. 370 (Review of *Philosophy of the Literary Symbolic* by Hazard Adams).

329 'Death on the Windy Dunes', *New York Times Book Review* (29 July), pp. 1, 32–3 (Review of *Tough Guys Don't Dance* by Norman Mailer).

330 'Foreigners', *London Review of Books* 6, no. 11 (21 June–4 July), pp. 11–12 (Review of *Selected Essays* by John Bayley, *Collected Poems* by Michael Hamburger, and *Poems: 1953–1983* by Anthony Thwaite).

331 'Golden Boy', *London Review of Books* 5, no. 24 (22 December 1983–18 January 1984), p. 22 (Review of *W. H. Auden: The Critical Heritage*, ed. John Haffenden, *Auden: A Carnival of Intellect* by Edward Callan, and *Drawn from the Life: A Memoir* by Robert Medley).

332 'A Mad Muse', *New Republic* 190, no. 30 (30 April), pp. 27–9 (Review of *Sweeney Astray: A Version from the Irish* by Seamus Heaney). Reprinted as 'Heaney's Sweeney', in *We Irish* (1986), pp. 267–71.

333 'Making Sense', *London Review of Books* 6, no. 18 (4

October), pp. 22–3 (Review of books by John Ashbery, Andrew Motion, Tom Paulin, Christopher Middleton, James Michie, Jeremy Reed, and George Mackay Brown).

334 'Morgan to his Friends', *London Review of Books* 6, nos 14–15 (2 August), p. 8 (Review of *Selected Letters of E. M. Forster, Volume 1: 1879–1920*, eds Mary Lago and P. N. Furbank).

335 'On the Text of *Ulysses*', *London Review of Books* 6, no. 17 (20 September), pp. 14–15 (Review of *Ulysses: A Critical and Synoptic Edition* by James Joyce, ed. Hans Walter Gabler, and *James Joyce* by Richard Ellmann). Reprinted in *We Irish* (1986), pp. 107–19.

336 'Plain English', *London Review of Books* 6, no. 24 (20 December), pp. 7–8 (Review of books on George Orwell and *Nineteen Eighty-Four*).

337 'Poets in their Places', *New Republic* 191, no. 25 (17 December), pp. 38–40 (Review of *T. S. Eliot: A Life* by Peter Ackroyd and *Saving Civilization: Yeats, Eliot, and Auden Between the Wars* by Lucy McDiarmid).

338 'The Return of the Native', *New York Review of Books* 31, no. 12 (19 July), pp. 32–4 (Review of *An American Procession* by Alfred Kazin).

339 'Textual Choices', *Times Higher Education Supplement* 605 (8 June), p. 20 (Review of *The Collected Poems of W. B. Yeats*, ed. Richard J. Finneran and *A New Commentary on the Poems of W. B. Yeats* by A. Norman Jeffares).

340 Review of *Towards 2000* and *Writing in Society* by Raymond Williams and *Radical Earnestness: English Social Theory 1880–1980* by Fred Inglis, *London Review of Books* 6, no. 2 (2–15 February), pp. 20–2. Reprinted as 'Raymond Williams'; in *England, Their England* (1988), pp. 351–8.

341 'With a Public in Mind', *Times Literary Supplement* 4249 (7 September), p. 987 (Review of *The Poet and His Audience* by Ian Jack).

1985

342 Afterword to *On the Shoulders of Giants: A Shandean Postscript* by Robert K. Merton (New York: Harcourt Brace Jovanovich, Vicennial Edition), pp. 291–300.

343 'The Fiction of James Joyce', in *The Genius of Irish Prose*, ed. Augustine Martin (Cork: Mercier Press), pp. 76–88. Reprinted as 'The European Joyce', in *We Irish* (1986), pp. 89–99.

344 'A Form of Attention', in *Creation and Interpretation*, eds Raphael Stern et al. (New York: Haven Publications), pp. 75–100.

345 '*Nineteen Eighty-Four:* Politics and Fable', in *George Orwell and Nineteen Eighty-Four: The Man and the Book*, Vol. 9 (Washington, D. C.: Library of Congress), pp. 57–69. Reprinted in *England, Their England* (1988), pp. 306–22.

346 'Attitudes toward History: A Preface to *The Sense of the Past*', *Salmagundi* 68–9 (Fall 1985–Winter 1986), pp. 107–24. Reprinted as 'Henry James and *The Sense of the Past*', in *Reading America* (1987), pp. 127–43.

347 'Newton's Other Law: Glory is the Real Reward', *New York Times Book Review* (21 April), p. 34.

348 'On "Gerontion"', *Southern Review* 21, no. 4 (Autumn), pp. 934–46. Reprinted in *Reading America* (1987), pp. 144–57.

349 'Alice, the Radical Homemaker', *New York Times Book Review* (22 September), pp. 3, 29 (Review of *The Good Terrorist* by Doris Lessing).

350 'An American Sage', *New York Review of Books* 32, no. 14 (26 September), pp. 39–42 (Review of *Attitudes Toward History* and *Permanence and Change: An Anatomy of Purpose* by Kenneth Burke). Reprinted as 'Kenneth Burke', in *Reading America* (1987), pp. 265–75.

351 'Just a Smack at Grigson', *London Review of Books* 7, no. 4 (7 March), p. 16 (Review of six books by Geoffrey Grigson).

352 'Keach and Shelley', *London Review of Books* 7, no. 16 (19 September), pp. 12–13 (Review of *Shelley's Style* by

William Keach and *Ariel: A Shelley Romance* by André Maurois and Ella D'Arcy). Reprinted as 'Shelley's Way', in *England, Their England* (1988), pp. 139–48.

353 'The Maze of Thought and Feeling', *Times Literary Supplement* 4271 (8 February), p. 139 (Review of books on Alexander Pope).

354 'A Myth and its Unmasking', *Times Literary Supplement* 4309 (1 November), pp. 1239–40 (Review of *Celtic Revivals: Essays in Modern Irish Literature* by Seamus Deane and *Ascendancy and Tradition in Anglo-Irish Literary History from 1789–1939* by W. J. McCormack).

355 'Owning Literature', *Raritan* 4, no. 4 (Spring), pp. 97–106 (Review of *The Force of Poetry* by Christopher Ricks).

356 'Portrait of a Critic', *New Republic* 192, no. 13 (1 April), pp. 29–33 (Review of new editions of *Essays on Literature; American Writers; English Writers* and *French Writers; Other European Writers; The Prefaces to the New York Edition* by Henry James).

357 'Raiding Joyce', *London Review of Books* 7, no. 7 (18 April), pp. 7–8 (Review of books on James Joyce).

358 'Reading Bakhtin', *Raritan* 5, no. 2 (Fall), pp. 107–19 (Review of *Mikhail Bakhtin: The Dialogical Principle* by Tzvetan Todorov, Wlad Godzich).

359 Review of *Selected Poems* by John Ashbery, *Boston Globe* (22 December), p. 13. Reprinted as 'John Ashbery III', in *Reading America* (1987), pp. 316–19.

360 'A Study in T. S. Eliot', *Southern Review* 21, no. 1 (Winter), pp. 178–82 (Review of *T. S. Eliot: A Study in Character and Style* by Ronald Bush).

361 'The Sublime Blackmur', *Antaeus* 55 (Autumn), pp. 287–98.

362 'Ten Poets', *London Review of Books* 7, no. 19 (7 November), pp. 20–2 (Review of books by Donald Davie, Allen Ginsberg, D. J. Enright, Edwin Morgan, Jeffrey Wainwright, Gillian Clarke, Richard Murphy, Sylvia Townsend Warner, and James Simmons).

363 'Venisti tandem', *London Review of Books* 7, no. 2 (7 February), pp. 18–19 (Review of books by Tony Harrison, Frederick Seidel, Andrew Motion, David Harsent, and Jaroslav Seifert).

1986

364   *We Irish: Essays on Irish Literature and Society* (New York: Knopf), ix, 275 pp. Reissued in paperback, 1988 (Berkeley and Los Angeles: University of California Press).

365   (Ed. with Introduction), *Selected Essays of R. P. Blackmur* (New York: Ecco Press), 372 pp.

366   'Emerson at First: A Commentary on *Nature*', in *Emerson and His Legacy: Essays in Honor of Quentin Anderson*, ed. Stephen Donadio et al. (Carbondale, Ill.: Southern Illinois University Press), pp. 23–47. Reprinted in *Reading America* (1987), pp. 20–39.

367   'The Sublime Blackmur', Introduction to *Selected Essays of R. P. Blackmur*, pp. 3–16.

368   'Yeats, Ancestral Houses, and Anglo-Ireland', in *Ascendancy Ireland*, ed. Franklin D. Murphy (Los Angeles: William Andrews Clark Library, University of California Press), pp. 33–52. Text of paper read at a Clark Library Seminar (28 September 1985). Reprinted in *We Irish*, pp. 52–66.

369   'A Criticism of One's Own', *New Republic* 194, no. 10 (10 March), pp. 30–4.

370   'The Promiscuous Cool of Postmodernism', *New York Times Book Review* (22 June), pp. 1, 36–7.

371   'Alexander Pope: Wit, Scholar, and Poet', *Washington Post Book World* 16, no. 6 (9 February), pp. 1, 8–9 (Review of *Alexander Pope: A Life* by Maynard Mack).

372   'Gentlemen Travellers', *London Review of Books* 8, no. 22 (18 December), p. 10 (Review of books on travel by Patrick Leigh Fermor, Jonathan Raban, and Hunter Davies).

373   'A Hero of Our Own Times', *New York Review of Books* 33, no. 11 (26 June), pp. 7–10 (Review of *A Man of Letters: Selected Essays* by V. S. Pritchett).

374   'The Limits of Language', *New Republic* 195, no. 1 (7 July), pp. 40–5 (Review of *The Resistance to Theory* by Paul de Man and *The Lesson of Paul de Man*, ed. Peter Brooks).

375   'A Man, a Woman, and a Blackbird', *New Republic* 195, no. 20 (17 November), pp. 46–8 (Review of *Wallace Stevens: A Biography, The Early Years, 1879–1923* by Joan

Richardson). Reprinted as 'Wallace Stevens', in *Reading America* (1987), pp. 218–24.

376 'A Poet of the Self and the Weather', *Times Literary Supplement* 4334 (25 April), pp. 435–6 (Review of books by Henry David Thoreau edited by Robert F. Sayre and *Writing Nature: Henry David Thoreau's Journal* by Sharon Cameron). Reprinted and abridged as 'Thoreau', in *Reading America* (1987), pp. 40–67.

377 'Ransom and Jarrell', *Partisan Review* 53, no. 1, pp. 126–32 (Review of books on the letters of John Crowe Ransom and Randall Jarrell).

378 'Shakers', *London Review of Books* 8, no. 19 (6 November), p. 22 (Review of *Write On: Occasional Essays '65 to '85* by David Lodge).

379 'Shakespeare in the Sonnets', *Raritan* 6, no. 1 (Summer), pp. 123–37 (Review of books on Shakespeare's *Sonnets*). Reprinted in *England, Their England* (1988), pp. 49–63.

380 'She's Got Rhythm', *New York Review of Books* 33, no. 19 (4 December), pp. 40–4 (Review of *The Complete Prose of Marianne Moore*, ed. Patricia C. Willis). Reprinted as 'Marianne Moore', in *Reading America* (1987), pp. 206–17.

381 'Was Swift a Monster?', *London Review of Books* 8, no. 10 (5 June), p. 12 (Review of *Jonathan Swift: A Hypocrite Reversed* by David Nokes).

382 'The Young Yeats', *New York Review of Books* 33, no. 13 (14 August), pp. 14–16 (Review of *The Collected Letters of W. B. Yeats, Volume 1, 1865–1895*, ed. John Kelly).

1987

383 *Reading America: Essays on American Literature* (New York: Knopf), xii, 320 pp. Reissued in paperback, 1988 (Berkeley and Los Angeles: University of California Press).

384 'Blackmur on Henry James', in *The Legacy of R. P. Blackmur: Essays, Memoirs, Texts*, ed. Joseph Frank et al. (New York: Ecco Press), pp. 21–43.

385 'Epireading and Graphireading', in *Issues in Contemporary Critical Theory*, ed. Peter Barry (London: Macmillan),

pp. 55–7. Extracts from *Ferocious Alphabets* (1981), pp. 146–8, 199–201.

386 'Walt Whitman', in *The New History of Literature: American Literature to 1900*, ed. Marcus Cunliffe (New York: Bedrick), pp. 227–51. Reprinted from 'Walt Whitman's Poetry', in *American Literature to 1900* (1973), pp. 258–86. Reprinted in *Reading America* (1987), pp. 68–96.

387 'Feelings of And and If, Of and But', *New York Times Book Review* (25 January), p.10.

388 'Seeking the Source of the Blaze', *NYU Magazine* 2 (Winter), pp. 50–5.

389 'Relax, It's Only a Theory', *New York Times Book Review* (1 March), p. 14.

390 'What Makes Life Worth Writing?' *New York Times Book Review* (29 March), pp. 11–12.

391 'Her Man Friday', *New York Times Book Review* (22 February), pp. 1, 26–7 (Review of *Foe* by J. M. Coetzee).

392 'Language and Loss', *New Republic* 197, no. 24 (14 December), pp. 34–8 (Review of *The Penguin Book of Modern Yiddish Verse*, ed. Irving Howe et al.).

393 'Louis MacNeice and the Thrusting of Shakespeare into Touch', *London Review of Books* 9, no. 8 (23 April), p. 19 (Review of *Selected Literary Criticism of Louis MacNeice*, ed. Alan Heuser).

394 'The Luck of the Irish', *New York Review of Books* 34, no. 3 (26 February), pp. 25–6 (Review of *The New Oxford Book of Irish Verse*, ed. Thomas Kinsella and *The Faber Book of Contemporary Irish Poetry*, ed. Paul Muldoon).

395 'Reading in the Dark', *Partisan Review* 54, no. 3, pp. 477–80 (Review of *Joyce's Book of the Dark: Finnegans Wake* by John Bishop).

396 'Whose Trope is it Anyway?', *New York Review of Books* 34, no. 11 (25 June), pp. 50–2 (Review of *The Renewal of Literature: Emersonian Reflections* by Richard Poirier).

1988

397 *England, Their England: Commentaries on English Language and Literature* (New York: Knopf), x, 365 pp. Reissued in

paperback, 1989 (Berkeley and Los Angeles: University of California Press).

398 (Ed. with Leslie Berlowitz and Louis Menand), *America in Theory* (New York and London: Oxford University Press), xvi, 302 pp.

399 'Modernism and its Canon', *The Southern Review and Modern Literature*, eds Lewis P. Simpson, James Olney, and Jo Gulledge (Baton Rouge: Louisiana State University Press), pp. 221–34.

400 'Swift and the Assocation of Ideas', in *Pope, Swift and Their Circle, Yearbook of English Studies* 18, ed. Claude Rawson (London: Modern Humanities Research Associates), pp. 1–17.

401 'The True Sentiments of America', in *America in Theory*, pp. 229–48.

402 'The Concept of the Avant-Garde', BBC Radio 3 (27 April).

403 'The Political Turn in Criticism', *Salmagundi* 81 (Winter), pp. 104–22.

404 'Yeats: The Daily Spite of This Unmannerly Town', BBC Radio 3 (10 May).

405 'Yeats and Modernism', *The World and I* 3, no. 6 (June), pp. 549–59.

406 'Domestic Muse', *New Republic* 199, no. 3 (18 July), pp. 38–41 (Review of *Nora: The Real Life of Molly Bloom* by Brenda Maddox).

407 'The Essential Posture', *New Republic* 199, no. 22 (28 November), pp. 28–31 (Review of *The Essential Gesture: Writing, Politics and Places* by Nadine Gordimer).

408 'Huston's Joyce', *New York Review of Books* 35, no. 3 (3 March), pp. 18–19 (Review of *The Dead*, a film by John Huston based on the story by James Joyce).

409 'In their Master's Steps', *Times Literary Supplement* 4472 (16 December), pp. 1399–1400 (Review of recently published works on literary criticism and theory).

410 'Insincerity and Authenticity', *New Republic* 198, no. 4 (15 February), pp. 25–32 (Review of *Oscar Wilde* by Richard Ellmann).

411 'One Life was not Enough', *New York Times Book Review* (17 January), pp. 1, 40 (Review of *Chatterton* by Peter

Ackroyd). Reprinted in as 'Chatterton', in *England, Their England*, pp. 359–63.

412 'Play it Again, Sam', *New York Review of Books* 35, no. 19 (15 December), pp. 30–5 (Review of Mike Nichols's production of *Waiting for Godot* by Samuel Beckett at the Lincoln Center, New York City).

413 'The Poet as Prizefighter', *Times Literary Supplement* 4465 (28 October), p. 1203 (Review of recently published books about Hugh MacDiarmid).

414 'The Poet in Limbo', *New York Review of Books* 35, no. 20 (22 December), pp. 45–8 (Review of *Conrad Aiken: Poet of White Horse Vale* by Edward Butscher).

415 'Pound's Book of Beasts', *New York Review of Books* 35, no. 9 (2 June), pp. 14–16 (Review of recently published critical works on Ezra Pound).

416 'Sean O'Casey: Life and Works', *New York Times Book Review* (3 July), p. 7 (Review of *Sean O'Casey: A Life* by Garry O'Connor).

417 'The Temptation of St. Tom', *New York Times Book Review* (16 October), pp. 1, 38–9 (Review of *Eliot's New Life* by Lyndall Gordon).

1989

418 'The Domestication of Outrage', in *The Symbolic Order*, ed. Peter Abbo (London: Falmer Press), pp. 104–11. Reprinted from *The Arts Without Mystery* (1983), pp. 31–41.

419 'Notes on a Later Poem by Stevens', in *Omnium Gatherum: Essays for Richard Ellmann*, eds Susan Dick, Declan Kiberd, Douglas McMillan, and Joseph Ronsley (Gerrards Cross: Colin Smythe), pp. 167–74.

420 'Translation in Theory and in a Certain Practice', in *The Art of Translation*, ed. Rosanna Warren (Boston: Northeastern University Press), pp. 244–57.

421 'Yeats and European Criticism', in *Yeats the European*, ed. A. Norman Jeffares (Gerrards Cross: Colin Smythe; Savage, Md.: Barnes and Noble) pp. 38–48.

422   'Blind Bitter Land', *Listener* 121, no. 3096 (12 January), pp. 6–7.

423   'The Strange Case of Paul de Man', *New York Review of Books* 36, no. 11 (29 June), pp. 32–7.

424   'T. S. Eliot's *The Idea of a Christian Society*', *Yale Review* 78, no. 2 (Winter), pp. 218–34.

425   'The Compleat Critic', *New Republic* 200, no. 25 (19 June), pp. 45–8 (Review of *I. A. Richards: His Life and Work* by John P. Russo).

426   'Haggling Presences', *New York Review of Books* 36, no. 14 (28 September), pp. 39–41 (Review of recently published translations from modern Hebrew).

427   'I Have Preened, I Have Lived', *New York Times Book Review* (5 March), p. 7 (Review of *Self-Consciousness: Memoirs* by John Updike).

428   'In a Personal Spirit', *Times Literary Supplement* 4487 (31 March), p. 331 (Review of *The Book of God: A Response to the Bible* by G. Josipovici).

429   'In the Celtic Twilight', *Times Literary Supplement* 4517 (27 October), pp. 1171–2 (Review of *No Laughing Matter: The Life and Times of Flann O'Brien* by A. Cronin).

430   'Ire Land', *New Republic* 201, no. 25 (18 December), pp. 37–9 (Review of *Ulster: Conflict and Consent* by Tom Wilson).

431   'Ireland, Whose Ireland?', *Wilson Quarterly* 13, no. 3 (Summer), pp. 88–90 (Review of *Modern Ireland: 1600–1972* by R. F. Foster).

432   'The Joy of Texts', *New Republic* 200, no. 26 (26 June), pp. 36–8 (Review of *The Pleasures of Reading in an Ideological Age* by Robert Alter).

433   'Making the Most of Dublin', *New York Times Book Review* (16 July), p. 3 (Review of *A Link with the River* by Desmond Hogan).

434   'Poetry and Sanity', *New Republic* 200, no. 10 (6 March), pp. 38–40 (Review of *A Serious Character: The Life of Ezra Pound* by Humphrey Carpenter and *The American Ezra Pound* by Wendy Flory).

435   'Principles and Intuitions', *Times Literary Supplement* 4483 (3 March), pp. 217–18 (Review of *The Company of Critics* by M. Walzer and *Resources of Hope* by R. Williams).

436 'The Revel's Ended', *New York Review of Books* 36, no. 5 (20 March), pp. 35–6 (Review of *Any Old Iron* by Anthony Burgess).

437 'The Sad Captain of Criticism', *New York Review of Books* 36, no. 3 (2 March), pp. 22–4 (Review of *Ruin the Sacred Truths: Poetry and Belief from the Bible to the Present* by Harold Bloom).

1990

438 *Warrenpoint* (New York: Knopf), 193 pp.

439 Introduction to *A Stanley Burnshaw Reader* by Stanley Burnshaw (Athens: University of Georgia Press), pp. xiii–xx.

440 'Going back to Pater and Wilde', in *Tensions and Transitions (1869–1990): The Mediating Imagination, for Ian Gregor*, eds Michael Irwin, Mark Kinkead-Weekes, and A. Robert Lee (London: Faber and Faber), pp. 27–46.

441 'I have never been able to tell a Story', *New York Times Book Review* (2 September), p. 1 (Excerpt from *Warrenpoint*).

442 'On "Thoreau on Paran Creek"', *Salmagundi* 87 (Summer), pp. 148–58.

443 'Portrait of the Critic as a Young Man', *Wilson Quarterly* 14, no. 3 (Summer), pp. 106–12.

444 'Pound's Joyce, Eliot's Joyce', in *James Joyce: The Artist and the Labyrinth*, ed. Augustine Martin (London: Ryan), pp. 293–312.

445 'Speaking to Whom', *In All Things: Religious Faith and American Culture*, ed. Robert J. Daly (Kansas City, Mo.: Sheed and Ward), pp. 147–55.

446 'Virtuality in Music', *The Quarterly* 14 (Summer).

447 'William Wetmore Story and His Friends: The Enclosing Fact of Rome', in *The Sweetest Impression of Life: The James Family and Italy* (New York: New York University Press), pp. 210–27.

448 'The Magical Muse', *New Republic* 203, no. 15 (10 October), pp. 37–8 (Review of *Haroun and the Sea of Stories* by Salman Rushdie).

449 'A Modern Hamlet?' *Wilson Quarterly* 14, no. 4 (Autumn),

pp. 88–91 (Review of *Coleridge: Early Visions* by Richard Holmes).

450   'Myths of Identity', *Times Literary Supplement* 4575 (7 December), p. 1324 (Reviews of recently published critical works on Irish writing).

451   'Safe in the Hands of the Uncanny', *New York Times Book Review* (8 April), p. 15 (Review of *Constancia, and Other Stories for Virgins* by Carlos Fuentes).

452   'The Visible and the Invisible', *New Republic* 202, no. 20 (14 May), pp. 40–5 (Review of *In the Western Night: Collected Poems 1965–90* by Frank Bidart).

453   'What can the Matter be?', *London Review of Books* 12, no. 7 (5 April), pp. 8–9. (Review of *Ulster Politics: The Formative Years, 1868–86* by B. M. Walker and *Ireland 1912–1985: Politics and Society* by J. J. Lee).

454   'A Worldly Philosopher', *Wilson Quarterly* 14, no. 2 (Spring), pp. 92–4 (Review of *The Examined Life: Philosophical Meditations* by Robert Nozick).

1991/1992

455   *Being Modern Together* (The Richard Ellmann Lectures) (Atlanta, Ga.: The Scholars Press, forthcoming).

456   'Notes on "The Flight from the City"', in *The Poetry of Irving Feldman* ed. Harold Schweizer (Lewisburg, Pa.: Bucknell University Press, 1992), pp. 167–85.

457   'Reading Irving Feldman's Poetry', in *The Poetry of Irving Feldman*, ed. Harold Schweizer (Lewisburg, Pa.: Bucknell University Press, 1992), pp. 149–66.

458   'The Revolt against Tradition', *Partisan Review* 58, no. 2 (Spring), pp. 294–8.

459   'Musil: The Man without Certainties', *Wilson Quarterly* 15, no. 2 (Spring), pp. 88–91 (Review of *Precision and Soul* by Robert Musil).

460   'On the White Strand', *London Review of Books* 13, no. 7 (4 April), pp. 17–18 (Review of *The Selected Letters of Jack B. Yeats*, ed. Robin Skelton).

461   'The Poet of Modern Life', *New York Review of Books* 38, no. 4 (14 February), pp. 22–4 (Review of recently published

translations of works by Charles Baudelaire and a biography of the poet).

462   'Witness to Folly', *New York Times Book Review* (16 June), pp. 14–15 (Review of *Our Age: English Intellectuals Between the World Wars—A Group Portrait* by Noel Annan).

Index